HOMESCHOOLING ON A BUDGET

JESSICA MARIE BAUMGARTNER

DEFIANCE PRESS
& PUBLISHING

Homeschooling on a Budget

First Edition: 2022

Printed in the United States of America

10 9 8 7 6 5 4 3 2 1

ISBN-13: 978-1-955937-33-7 (Paperback)
ISBN-13: 978-1-955937-32-0 (eBook)

Published by Defiance Press and Publishing, LLC

Bulk orders of this book may be obtained by contacting Defiance Press and Publishing, LLC. www.defiancepress.com.

Public Relations Dept. – Defiance Press & Publishing, LLC
281-581-9300
pr@defiancepress.com

Defiance Press & Publishing, LLC
281-581-9300
info@defiancepress.com

DEDICATION

FOR MY ENERGETIC KIDS, MY EXHAUSTED HUSBAND,
AND ALL THE FAMILIES WHO ENJOY LEARNING.

Never stop learning!! ♥

*Jessica Marie
Baumgartner*

TABLE OF CONTENTS

INTRODUCTION

Homeschooling has become a popular term. It's a buzzword. It's everywhere, and there are many opinions on home education's place in society. Despite plenty of support, there are still many misconceptions about homeschooling. Thankfully, since it has gained so much popularity in recent decades, even the naysayers are finding less and less to argue against, as children educated by their parents excel in life. They have won spelling bees, graduated early, and gone on to be happy, healthy, productive members of society.

My children have only known homeschooling. It was not the original plan. When my eldest started nearing preschool age, my family lived in an urban area. By the time my daughter was ready for school, our district, the Normandy School District in St. Louis, Missouri, had lost its accreditation—meaning that the children there were receiving a sub-par education that was no longer meeting government standards.

I didn't want to leave the community. Both of my daughters were home-birthed in our cute little brick house. We had a giant backyard and nice neighbors, and our public library and favorite playground were within walking distance.

For the first time in my life, I considered homeschooling. The idea was foreign to me. I only knew of one person who had been homeschooled and that was a horror story. It was my cousin. Her parents had addiction issues and hastily pulled her out of public school because she was fighting with another child. Instead of resolving the conflict, they just avoided it. This taught her to run away from her problems.

I do not believe that homeschooling is a solution to individualized conflict, bullying, or every educational issue. I would not have reacted the same way in that situation, and my cousin did not grow up to be as healthy and well-adjusted as some would want her to. She has turned to crime, been to jail, and avoids family events.

This is the outcome that most people fear when they oppose home education options, and the concerns are valid. There are extreme cases where parents aren't teaching or offering a stable situation, but that happens to public school children as well. My father's alcoholism and my mother's inability to balance our home life highly affected my ability to focus and flourish when I went to public school. Now that I know multiple homeschooling families, I have found that the frightening cases are a rarity, but having had a negative homeschooling example in my life for so long, I use that to remind myself of how bad things can get if my husband and I don't work hard to give our children the best education possible.

Plenty of people still scoff at homeschoolers, though. I've yet to find anyone who questions my ability to teach; instead, they express concern for socialization and the "financial burden." It took a lot of research and testing myself to gain the confidence I needed to homeschool. It was our only viable option, as the public education system had already failed the children of our area. Socialization could be easily carried out in youth activity groups at the park, library events, and family get-togethers. The only real concern that remained prominent from my perspective was the "financial burden."

Everyone seemed to believe that homeschooling would cost a fortune. They truly thought that because the public education system required tens of thousands of dollars per student, it would cost that much to properly educate a child at home. This left me feeling inadequate. I knew I could teach my daughters everything they would learn from pre-school through grade school. I wasn't even that concerned about the coming middle-school years, and I had graduated high school and college, so I had to have at least some kind of ability to impart what I learned, and there were plenty of books and online resources to help me re-familiarize myself with all the material, but the cost of the materials is what really scared me.

Thankfully, there are wonderful networks of homeschoolers and homeschooling groups that publish and openly share their experiences, tips, and successes. I found plenty of encouragement in a few online searches. Homeschool conventions, stores, and websites seemed to be popping up everywhere too. There were plenty of resources for parents like me.

Homeschoolers nowadays have more teaching resources than ever. It has never been easier to teach a child at home. I also learned that most home educators set their own budgets. Public schools have to worry about strict regulations and preparing for rigorous tests (that really only teach children how to memorize material to get the correct answer and then move on instead of real-life applications). They have so many children to care for that funds are spent quickly, and children are *still* hit with a long list of supplies that families are expected to purchase before the school year starts.

Gaining some knowledge of homeschooling success stories helped me seek out different materials. I knew that I learned best through trial-and-error, experiments, and hands-on activities, so that's where I started with my eldest. I purchased a few affordable workbooks on letters, shapes, and colors, along with some fun craft kits and set to it. My daughter took to it like a puppy playing fetch. She loved school. She appreciated learning because it was fun, and when she had a bad day, I could sympathize and help her through it.

The main goal was to make learning enjoyable. The more I customized each day's work to my daughter's interests, the easier she learned. She loved ballet, so we danced while counting. We read ballet books and even celebrated correct answers with twirls. These individualized learning triumphs gave her the confidence to face new concepts with ease, and it led me to love homeschooling.

Her sister was completely different. She wasn't as girly and only cared about animals and drawing. I had to rework the lesson structure to keep her attention because she's an active child who doesn't like to sit still for long periods of time. I'm the same way. So, we incorporated more movement. If she got frustrated, I let her have stretching breaks or do jumping jacks to focus on something else for a few minutes.

She also loved drawing from the start. To reward her for applying herself, I let her draw cats and dogs all over her worksheets, bring a stuffed animal to class, and sometimes we brought our dog into the room, so my daughter could explain what she was learning to her favorite animal. Each kid is different, and keeping their interest is a challenge, but it doesn't cost much.

I quickly realized how wrong people had been about the costs of homeschooling. We didn't need fancy toys or expensive software to enjoy the learning process. All we needed was an appreciation of each other and a good budget. Buying some fun stickers to put on an A+ worksheet is highly affordable.

After over ten years of homeschooling, with now four children, I've learned as much as my kids have, if not more. That is a lesson in itself: that life is a constant learning experience and lessons don't start and stop in a classroom. I recently got dragged into a long online conversation with a group of people who truly thought that homeschooling was expensive and that only rich white people could successfully do it. There was also a note of disdain for Christian homeschoolers since religious extremism can be bred at home. Nearly every one of these opinions came from individuals who didn't have children—or liberal parents who were taught that public education is the only way for a child to properly gain their understanding of the world.

Their perception is based on outdated views of homeschooling. Black homeschooling families are gaining popularity. Homeschooling doesn't have a color, and good parents know that. My family is a religious minority. I am not a Christian, but my mother is and my family is spiritual, so I respect and appreciate parents who wish to allow their faith into their lessons because I believe in religious freedom and the right to exercise it. I came from a poor background, and though I can squeeze a dollar out of a dime,

I've never been incredibly wealthy (well, at least in the monetary sense).

Most of the families I've met who homeschool do not receive the benefits of being "privileged." They are often lower-middle-class or low-class families, and one of my best friends is a black mother who homeschooled her daughter through early education and then enrolled her into private school as she got older. There is no one-size-fits-all learning strategy that works for everyone. Parents don't have to homeschool through all ages and stages, just as not all kids have to stick to just public school or just private school from pre-school through college.

After my long online discussion displaying the reality of homeschooling costs, and how many "poor" or "underprivileged" individuals can and do homeschool, I decided to write this book. There are plenty of texts that lay out "how to homeschool," and though I will offer some of those details, that is not the main goal of this work. This title was expressly written to prove that homeschooling can be done by anyone regardless of income level.

It takes practice and organization. Parents have to work together and set clear, attainable goals, but in doing so, they can take control of their children's education, and cater it to each child's specific needs thus producing a more positive view of learning at a small fraction of the price that public schools take from tax revenue.

THE COSTS OF PUBLIC SCHOOL

Homeschooling on a budget isn't difficult. Parents handle the funds and materials and disperse them directly. There is no lengthy funneling of money to this department or that department. That alone cuts a lot of costs.

The public education system is funded through various channels. According to the Public-School Review (1), somewhere around 48 percent is funded through state revenue such as state income tax, sales tax, and other fees. Another 44 percent is funded through more localized revenue, mainly property taxes, and then on top of that, another 8 percent is federally funded through grants for specialized programs. With taxes constantly rising, and standards continuing to fall, it's not difficult for parents to step back and wonder why teachers and politicians constantly claim that public education still needs more funding. It also makes a number of us wonder if these funds are being properly managed when long lists of school supplies are expected to be purchased by the parents each year, the national average public school teacher's salary is above $60,000 a year (2), and the average school district superintendent salary is over $165,000 (3).

There is so much parents could do with money like that. Homeschooling parents could establish their own schools with that kind of money. Misappropriation of funds has been a growing concern for years, but it's difficult to prove and convict in many cases being that parents aren't involved in the auditing processes, nor are they handed a breakdown list of every public-school expense their tax dollars pay for. How can anyone fully "follow the money" if it's flowing in and out of the system like toilet paper?

And how do some publicly-funded schools fall so far behind that they lose their accreditation? Mismanagement is usually blamed, but what exactly does that mean? The details are so elusive that parents are often left in the dark.

If a school is funded by taxes and taxes are regularly collected, yet somehow the schools are still hurting, one cannot help but conclude that somewhere along the way the funding isn't being properly handled to meet students' needs. It is their needs that should always come first.

So let's check the price tag of a public education per child. According to the US Census Bureau's most recent findings, public schools spent an average of $12,201 for each student in attendance (4). By contrast, the 2022 Public School Review Report (5) revealed that Utah had the lowest average spending set at $8,830 per student, and New York had the highest, which is a whopping $38,270 per student. When reviewing their numbers state by state, the national average cost per public school student is over $15,000.

With all of that money, a parent could send their kid to private school where they would potentially receive a more thorough education, especially given the current climate of the public system. Politics and special interests are now dominating what children are taught and even how they are taught in public schools.

A perfect example was demonstrated during the COVID-19 pandemic. Powerful teachers' unions were exposed in advising the CDC on pandemic protocols during the COVID-19 outbreak (6), numerous teachers and school officials have been caught pandering inappropriate lessons and including one-sided politics in their curriculum, while standardized testing, and other insufficiencies continue to hinder learning, college readiness, and proper training for society and the workforce.

When news broke that the most powerful teachers' union, the American Federation of Teachers, sent specific language to the CDC director, Rochelle Walensky—and even included the White House in these email correspondences—to determine school re-openings during the COVID-19 pandemic, shock and confusion struck many parents. Even as a homeschooling mother, I wondered, *If we're worried about public health, then why is the CDC (the American government's top health organization) taking orders from a teachers' organization instead of the other way around? When my children are sick, I don't take them to a teacher to diagnose the issues and get the best medical care; I take them to a doctor.*

This situation exposed a lot of political bias that teachers' unions harbor, and how they use their influence to impose their ideologies onto our children by pressuring top experts, and legal officials into carrying out their orders. The pandemic opened a lot of people's eyes. Parents everywhere suddenly had to be more involved in their children's education, and they realized just how far behind the system has fallen, and just how it is veering down dangerous paths.

When the schools closed and remained so for extended periods, I had neighbors and friends apologizing to me for past their scrutiny. They asked for advice, and many of them questioned where public education funds are going because they were able to help their kids finish their lessons in half the time that public schools taught before the shutdowns. It is a valid question. If kids can learn faster at home, without as much time or money, then are public schools serving the community properly?

From my experiences as a child who went through the public school system, I witnessed how it started slowly degrading for years. Instead of focusing on studies and preparing students for the real world, the main goal shifted from core lessons and knowledge on various subjects to socializing children and teaching them to do as they're told. Critical thinking was left behind and replaced with common core after my time, and so now logic and critical thinking have taken a back seat to progressive ideals that promote obedience and mob mentality over students thinking for themselves and learning the proper skills to become self-reliant.

Yes, children need to learn to follow the rules and apply themselves. Sometimes, adults have to work in groups, but everyone also needs the freedom to explore different ideas, topics, and events if they are going to better themselves and figure out what kind of life they need to lead. Teachers' unions seem to have forgotten this.

Many people join the teaching profession because they want to mold young minds and make the world a better place. It is a noble cause that can help others and lead to a fulfilling life, but some teachers allow this to overinflate their egos. They take that sense of purpose too far and cross boundaries that should not be crossed in the classroom. They are also forced to pay union dues and uphold union ideologies, so their ability to serve the children becomes more easily

corrupted. At this point, it should be common knowledge that teachers' unions, and even teachers themselves, are generally more liberal.

This is not a bad thing if teachers, unions, and schools remember the children first, above all else. Unfortunately, conservative and even moderate parents are finding this isn't the case anymore. Parents are literally paying taxes to fund public schools that push liberal ideologies. The idea of public schooling is a more liberal concept, so it makes logical sense and has the potential for positive outcomes when properly balanced. That balance has been tipped and spilled over, as teachers and schools are now openly allowing their politics to lead them into teaching harmful materials without consulting parents or even responding when parents speak out.

For example, a Florida school board member took an elementary school class on a paid field trip to a gay bar that served a menu full of foods with sexual titles (7). It may be a fun novelty for adults, but it is not for children, nor should it be. There are plenty of other ways to teach acceptance and understanding of people who deviate from norms than flat-out desensitizing minors to sex and vulgarity.

Another example of this kind of political overreach stems from a California teacher who removed the American flag and replaced it with the LGBTQ pride flag and encouraged children to pledge to it instead (8). Again, people can love their country *and* be respectful of others' rights. Maybe she didn't understand why students pledge to our nation's flag, but homeschooling parents do. The entire purpose of a national anthem is to unify people from all backgrounds. Like many countries, it is a symbol of the people. Whether the LGBTQ community agrees, the American flag represents them too. In our country, it is also a reminder that the United States is governed by the people and for those people.

The pride flag does not represent a country. It is exclusionary and therefore not something that represents everyone, especially not children in a classroom who are not physically or mentally ready to explore their sexuality. This teacher's actions are curious because she used school time, which she is paid during (via the people's taxes), to try and sway her students to follow her beliefs, not the curriculum.

In addition, BLM flags have been allowed in schools (9) to support the Black Lives Matter organization, while Back the Blue sentiments are suppressed (10). But this isn't even the main concern of parents dropping public school for homeschooling in regards to questionable practices being implemented by teachers in classrooms. Fairfax County Public Schools came under fire in 2021 for allowing genderqueer material with pornographic depictions into the school library (11) for the sake of "diversity and inclusion."

Many parents are all for being kind, respecting others' rights, and allowing people to be themselves, but when a school allows sexual content into their library—for minors who are not legally able to consent to sexual activity—it is a red flag. The sexualization of minors has become commonplace in Hollywood and the media. It isn't anyone but a parent's job to censor these materials as they see fit because we don't fund Hollywood projects or even media communications, but we do fund public schools. There is no option for homeschoolers or parents of private schoolchildren to opt out of paying for these public institutions.

If we are paying to keep these schools stocked and running, then we deserve to know what children are being exposed to and have a say in making sure that kids are not being groomed for sexual abuse or sexual activity before they are ready (12). Grooming is often how children are lured into accepting molestation because they are primed to trust their abuser.

Lately, public-school policies on transgenderism are reaching the boundaries of grooming. A girl can no longer just be a tomboy without a counselor pulling her aside to discuss the possibility that the child may be trans. Boys can't possibly want to wear a dress for fun; they must be a trans girl by public-school rhetoric. It's a touchy subject—one that is very personal. Children like to test their boundaries, and some rare children actually have body dysphoria, but there are now multiple court cases filed against public school districts—from California (13) to Wisconsin (14) to Florida (15)—where parents are suing teachers for coaxing their children into transitioning to the opposite sex without parental consent or even the parent's knowledge.

This deceit is funded by us. And it's building a lack of trust because parents can't even know that their children are going to school to be taught math, science, English, and history. Now, they're being taught to question their identity, whether it is a personal concern or not.

Public schools receive tens of thousands of dollars per kid each year, to do this. They impart their politics, their beliefs, and their prejudices. School lunches are still sub-par, as are the curriculums. In some states, reading and math standards are being lowered or even erased (16) while students' skills are still measured by standardized tests that have little to no real-world correlations.

Test-taking is a skill, yes. I struggled with it as a child, so it's important to me that my children know how to sit and focus and fill in the blanks and bubbles, but it's not how I measure their intelligence. As I've taught through the years, I've learned that my children display what they've learned best through action, teaching others themselves, storytelling, practical application projects, and art.

Meanwhile, in public schools, students have to take remedial classes or transition courses (17) just to enter college at the standard level. In February of 2022, it was reported that 77 percent of Baltimore high school students were reading at an elementary school level (18). This is what the Department of Education is doing with our money?

This may be a direct result of the fact that many public schools no longer hold students back if they cannot keep up, nor do they allow children who excel to skip a grade. My eldest started school two years ahead and has kept a steady pace. She wants to graduate early, and I'm happy to accommodate that.

A couple of years ago, we were considering public school because her father and I got a divorce and we moved away, but when I contacted the new school district, they had no interest in placing her where she was meant to be. I asked if they could test her skills or if I could provide proof that she was ahead of her peers. The secretary straight-up said, "That's just too much paperwork. We don't do that anymore." I was offered the potential to enroll her in a gifted program (19), where she would receive extra work. She was upset and asked, "Why do they want to punish me for being smart?"

Her response struck me. I thought, "Should smarter kids have to work harder and receive the same treatment? Of course not." Needless to say, I kept homeschooling (which was difficult because I had taken a full-time writing job, but it worked out).

On the opposite end, a friend of mine had a younger sister struggling through her elementary school classes. She fell so far behind that her mother was begging the school to hold her back. She just wasn't ready. Some kids need more time. The school refused. And the child continued to suffer. She now hates school.

My youngest daughter is not as advanced as my eldest. She is dyslexic, like me, and would most likely suffer under public school policies. It doesn't help knowing that her aunt was a straight-A student in high school, who went to college immediately after graduation, yet she needed to take remedial math classes because her A+ knowledge was still below the requirement for college algebra.

Everywhere, I hear stories about children struggling in the public system and adults who are unhappy with the results. Especially after how public schoolchildren were dehumanized and treated like germ factories during the pandemic (20). Yet, still so many people refuse to pull their kids from these toxic institutions because they can't afford private school, and they don't have enough faith in themselves to homeschool.

They've been told that a good education is expensive. It's not. A good education requires being attentive to each child's strengths, interests, and goals. Anyone can teach, and they can do it with affordable materials. They don't need thousands of dollars because when a child has fun learning, they'll work as hard as they can. Even on bad days, they understand the need so long as the parents openly encourage them and express why it's important to gain knowledge and seek wisdom.

The costs of public school are not just monetary. As high as those are, when shipping children off to these schools, parents have little to no control over the values, politics, and subjects being taught. As critical race theory replaces history class, reading and math standards are lowered to accommodate children who should probably receive more help or one-on-one tutoring, and teachers openly talk down to parents and push radical political ideologies like embracing communism, the stakes are much higher than we could ever calculate. The price tag isn't just your tax dollars: it includes your children's faith, respect, and future.

THE COSTS OF HOMESCHOOLING

Now that we've laid out the long list of monetary, mental, emotional, and political costs of public education, it's time to dig into the truth about homeschooling. So many people are wondering how much homeschooling costs. What are the success rates? And do homeschooled children do as well as children who've been through the public education system?

The answers vary, but they aren't as broad as some parents suspect. When I first started homeschooling, I spent a couple hundred dollars a year on my daughter. Pre-school and kindergarten are pretty easy, it turns out.

We had plenty of materials at home already. Books, art supplies, a big backyard, and a love of learning gave me the confidence I needed to lead my daughter through her early education, and it helped her have fun and crave knowledge. School was something we looked forward to and still do.

As she matured into more challenging courses and her sister began her lessons, the elementary school costs grew to about $500 a year. This is including field-trips and everything. After my divorce and remarriage, this baseline price tag has remained constant even as my eldest son begins his home education. Due to increasing inflation rates (21), I anticipate that this may need to be raised by one or two hundred dollars in the coming years, but it is such a small fraction of the average public school price.

By homeschooling, my family spends less than four percent of the funds that the current public education system would spend for each of my children. Imagine saving ninety-six percent of your tax dollars if homeschooling were a deduction. Unfortunately, it is not, and so my husband and I grudgingly accept that the portion of our money, which is taken for the public education system—that we do not utilize—is a forced donation.

Maybe someday, homeschooling parents will receive the tax breaks they deserve for their work and dedication, but for now, it is not the case. Still, my family is not alone. The average homeschooler spends between $500 and $1,000 on each of their children per school year (22).

It is a new concept for many parents, especially people who were raised in the public education system and led to believe that public schooling is free. These are the same people who express support for "free" college, not realizing that their "free" college tuition, if implemented, will cost them plenty. The department of education is already struggling to appease parents of elementary school students, I can't imagine what kind of dissent they would meet should they fail a generation of college kids who were promised a good public college education and feel that they have been cheated.

As Margaret Thatcher once said, "There is no such thing as public money; there is only taxpayers' money." This sentiment has been rebranded through social media memes and conservative public sentiments, reminding Americans that, "There is no such thing as government-funded. There is only taxpayer-funded."

Many parents seem to have forgotten that they *do* pay for public schools and therefore own them and should have some element of control as to how the funding is spent. Budgets are hard. They're long slopes of numbers that threaten to ski off cliffs every time you check them, but a careful hand and close monitoring can keep everything on track.

It takes patience and planning. Instead of sitting back and letting someone else handle the funds, homeschooling parents directly pay for everything. We can trace every dollar, every cent. That makes a huge difference when you're spending money on a child's education.

At the start of the year, between January and March, I start researching new materials and look at what we've already used, then assess if we want to stick with the same line of workbooks, if my kids are excelling with certain websites, and so on. I give myself a strict $500 budget per child and slowly determine what we need and see if we can afford extras here and there. I do this in the spring so that when my husband and I file our tax returns and receive our child tax credits, we can apply what we get back into our children's education. Having four kids already means we have to keep a close watch on our finances. Just feeding and clothing them and finding good sports/art programs takes planning and saving up money.

My family is not rich. With my uncertain writing career, and my husband working for tips, we make a combined annual income of around $40,000. That may seem like a lot to a single person fresh out of college, but when supporting four kids, it's tight.

I consider it a thrilling challenge. Playing with numbers doesn't have to be work. Just as I teach my children that their lessons can be fun, I try to enjoy working the budget. It's like a puzzle. I just need to fit in the materials that work and pick and choose what we'd like to test out for the upcoming school year.

Once everything has been acquired, I set it in storage until August. My children start their school year the day after Labor Day, just like I did when I was a kid and their grandparents did. Sitting down to lay out each day's lessons and stack and record them is work. It takes time and effort in addition to the money spent, but the care and effort that my husband and I give to our children's education is repaid with their hard work.

It allows us to be self-reliant, so we don't have to take snow days or worry about other weather conditions. During the pandemic, my children's lives were not disrupted. We carried on as usual and that sense of normalcy helped them through the frustration when certain friends couldn't come over to play or specific stores and community facilities were closed.

Because we make our own budget, we can implement classes that most schools don't have, like gardening. I don't know how many children are learning how to grow their own food anymore, but I consider it a vital resource. Again, during the pandemic, it was our vegetable garden and the Farmer's Market that helped relieve some of the financial burden. Now that inflation has followed, I look to the fruit trees we planted in 2020 and know that the lessons my kids are learning are more sustainable than a lot of what they would learn in a public education setting.

Our physical education classes are also more practical. We don't have to spend any money buying special gym shorts or vests. Instead of making physical activity some kind of classroom experience, we allow the children to incorporate it into their daily routine like adults do. Some days, we dance to music, others we take a three-mile hike. We each have our own yoga mat. Playing tag at the playground or jumping rope are also fun ways we get exercise, and these varying methods teach my children that being active isn't something you have to force yourself to do; it's a good way to have fun *and* stay in shape.

Giving children options helps them make decisions for themselves. They take the initiative and learn self-reliance. This is another free by-product of homeschooling.

You can't buy resourcefulness, but you can display it. As a parent *and* a teacher, I openly discuss my own concerns when someone loses the markers or pops a ball. The children are taught to value every teaching tool we own because we pay for it, and when it needs to be replaced, that comes directly out of our pockets.

These are lessons that children need to learn. They cannot run around being handed everything without ever knowing the cycle of cause-and-effect that makes for a well-rounded education. It seems that sometimes public educators underestimate children or assume their abilities for them and ignore or gloss over these life lessons.

At home, because I offer more insight, my children openly tell me what kind of goals they want to achieve and receive direct one-on-one encouragement. This means my husband and I can customize lessons for individualized interests.

When I'm working on our budget and planning for the next year, the books and lessons I research and acquire are based on each child's interests. My eldest daughter loved ballet when she was little, but she grew out of that after nine years of dance. Now she's more focused on sewing and wishes to make beautiful dresses. Because of this, I have incorporated a sewing class for her and added funds for patterns, fabric, and other sewing supplies into the budget.

Knowing how to sew a button onto a shirt, cook, clean up after one's self, and cultivate the land are all important things to know and use throughout life. Balancing budgets and bank accounts is vital to financial success. Having the ability to teach this as my kids grow assures me that they will be better off than children who know nothing of these subjects when they reach adulthood.

How I teach everything is as important as what is taught. Keeping students' attention is vital to their success. Many kids have trouble focusing in school as they get older and the material grows more difficult. Helping a child connect their interests to what their learning is the key to imparting knowledge. I learned this best from my other daughter.

My youngest daughter is obsessed with animals. She has trouble focusing at times, so to help her stay engaged in our lessons each day, my husband or I turn her math problems into stories about toads or frogs. We assign projects and lessons that encourage her interests. She's currently reading Joy Adamson's ever-popular Born Free series. She loves watching documentaries about animals and did a letter-writing project to Winter, the famous dolphin at the Clearwater Marine Aquarium. After Winter passed away, we adopted her friend Hope and studied dolphins.

My eldest son, who is just now in pre-school, loves animals too, but he's obsessed with the color red and he loves to draw. We allow him to trace letters and do his little worksheets with a red marker. Computer time is all about looking for the color red in his math and word games. Also, at the end of every lesson, to reward him for paying attention, he gets to draw whatever he wants.

These little things matter. They make all the difference, and most of them cost little to nothing. When you write your own budget, you can cut something here to add a little more somewhere else or splurge if someone gets a raise. Taking control of your child's education is well worth it, and best of all, you can teach good manners and values as well as share in community volunteer work for electives.

Parents who have a strong faith can incorporate their religious or spiritual beliefs into electives or other areas so long as the core classes are the main focus. The requirements vary state by state (23).

It is a more connected form of teaching. Parents are more invested in their children, so those who take the extra time to homeschool build even stronger ties with their children. That is another added benefit that costs nothing.

Each child's success is the true reward, but success stories properly display the value of budgeting and teaching children at home. Homeschooled children have been winning spelling bees and other national academic competitions for years; these included twenty-three homeschooled kids competing as finalists at the Scrips National Spelling Bee in 2019 (24). In 2021, Zaila Avant-garde made history when she became the first black student to win the Scrips National Spelling Bee, and of course, she is homeschooled by her parents (25).

Throughout much of history, homeschooling has been a preferred method of education, and it is still producing positive results. Abraham Lincoln, Pierre Curie, and Albert Einstein are historical figures who were educated at home (26). Modern athletes and artists like Simone Biles, Misty Copeland, Venus and Serena Williams, Selena Gomez, and Emma Watson were all homeschooled as well (27).

Before openly vocalizing my support and experiences homeschooling, I had no idea just how many people were finding success through this education route, but once I opened up, I came to learn that some of my friends and acquaintances were homeschooled, and I found a commonality between all of them. These were the politest individuals I knew, and they all seemed to value their interactions with others more.

I was shocked when I learned that a friend of mine was homeschooled. She never spoke about it but was happy to open up when I started teaching my eldest at home. I laughed and joked, saying, "See, and you're not weird."

She did admit, "Oh I was, but it wasn't a bad thing." When she went to college, it was a bit of an adjustment. She immediately realized that she was more connected to her family than most of the other students, and she wasn't as outspoken or angry at people who didn't agree with her.

That is one of the true costs of homeschooling. Our children are not as careless with their relationships, and so may feel a bit different or more emotionally mature, but I find that a benefit as well. Homeschooling isn't for everyone, but anyone who truly wants to teach their children at home can do it with hard work and patience, and they can lead their kids to success. That starts with a good budget.

Budgets are the foundation of teaching at home. They set boundaries and give parents the direction they need to embark on their journey as educators.

Staying within budget is a constant balance, but it pushes parents to work within their community as well. To cut costs, libraries, conventions, the Internet, and other great resources are available to anyone who seeks them. If the budget is the foundation of teaching, the tools that translate each lesson are the walls. They block out harsh winds but also welcome others in. This helps homeschooled children socialize as they grow into happy, intelligent adults.

UTILIZING LIBRARIES

ublic libraries have served a broad range of people for ages. They contain reference books, new releases, and free Internet access. Even private libraries serve to aid those who gain access to historical literature.

When I was a child, going to the library was magical. My mother took us often because my love of reading could not be quenched. My sister always needed to find books for research papers, and getting out together to visit a quiet place that catered to families offered a comfortable destination that appeased us all.

The Internet boom didn't really take off until I was in middle school, and we didn't have a computer in the home until I was a teenager. Just a generation ago, homeschooling seemed impossible. Home educators didn't have the massive resources that are available in the technological age.

Even parents of public schoolchildren, like my mother, relied on school and public libraries to help us with homework and guide us through our education. Walls of books called to me. Shelf after shelf held mystery and adventure.

I found my love of creative nonfiction on those shelves when I discovered the inspirational true story of Joy Adamson's tale in *Born Free*. Books like hers led me to seek out other true stories like *Little Rascal*, by

Sterling North, and *Freedom Train*, the story of Harriet Tubman.

Each of these works taught me history better than anything I learned in school. To this very day, I seek a better understanding of history and humanity from personal nonfiction stories. Tales like Ishmael Bea's *A Long Way Gone* and Abby Johnson's *Unplanned* are stories I wish to share with my children as they mature.

Without libraries, I would not have found these tales. Without them, I would never be the writer or teacher I am today.

Libraries are essential to homeschoolers. They offer free materials or low-cost printing so parents can duplicate references and properly lay out lessons that will stay with their children throughout their lives.

Checking out new books gets children excited to read and learn. Allowing them the freedom to pick out some of their own reading material teaches them how to take the initiative and learn something outside of the planned curriculum, without emptying your wallet. It also lends parents the ability to keep current with national standards and check up on what's popular.

Because the publishing industry has changed so quickly due to eBook and audiobook popularity, I do look through each title that my children pick up before allowing them to check the work out. Very rarely do I find materials that I think are inappropriate for children being marketed for them, but I have found that most popular children's books have more pictures and fewer words than ever.

There are even children's picture books with no words at all and a whole market that celebrates this. The Scholastic book company explained this (28) phenomenon as such: "Wordless picture books are valuable tools for literacy development, as they engage children, regardless of reading level, in prediction, critical thinking, meaning-making and storytelling."

That philosophy has led news outlets like The Washington Post (29), and even parenting (30) publications (31) to celebrate wordless books for children. It may be a well-intentioned sentiment, but it also forgets the point of books entirely: to translate thought into words that can be reproduced and shared throughout generations. They are meant to impart information, knowledge, and wisdom.

Illustrations were originally added into stories to offer imaginations a slight nudge, not develop the entire picture. The point of picture books is for parents and teachers to teach children to read by reading to them and displaying just how valuable written communication and verbal interpretation are. If you drop the need for verbal skills entirely, it leads underdeveloped minds to think they don't need to read.

It also "dumbs them down" so to speak. The rising popularity of wordless picture books caught on so well that it's been bleeding into later reading categories. Modern early readers, children's chapter books, and even middle-grade books have more pictures and fewer words than ever.

A fusion between classic writing and comic books has created a rift in the publishing world. More traditional readers, like myself, understand that comics and illustrated stories have their place, but we do not consider them the same things as literature. The ever-popular adult graphic novel *Watchmen* by Alan More is a brilliant story, but I do not place it at the same level as *Jane Eyre,* or *The Grapes of Wrath*, just as I do not compare those books to ancient works that were originally passed down through the oral tradition of storytelling, like *The Iliad* and *The Odyssey.*

Unfortunately, plenty of literary agents and even top publishers disagree. They proudly declare the *Dogman* series as a great work of children's literature and produce comic versions of best-selling series like the *Wings of Fire* books. Now, I love all literature and art, but classrooms are filled with children's chapter books that are glorified comics with less vocabulary substance and more "escapism" via pictures.

Graphic novel chapter books are being used to promote literacy in public schools as reading skills continue to suffer and drop. Meanwhile, homeschooling parents are teaching their children to use their own imaginations and appreciate that books without pictures are much more valuable than those without words.

Children who like to read don't like being handed simple material. Children who don't like to read don't want to feel stupid. Most kids who struggle with reading do so, not because the words are difficult, but because they don't care about the content. Adding pictures won't change that.

When I first started homeschooling we lived next door to a little boy who wasn't reaching his full potential in school. He was being raised by his grandmother and when I discussed his learning issues with her, she proudly stated that "He's only allowed to read the bible."

This shocked me. Instilling our beliefs in our children and grandchildren is a wonderful thing, but religious texts are difficult for adults to read and interpret; I can't imagine how frustrating it must have been for this grade-school-aged boy to try and pay attention and understand a book full of metaphors that were translated from ancient languages. He hated reading. He wanted nothing to do with it. So, when he got to school, he had no interest in any the materials they offered. He shut down. Kids do that when they feel stupid or are forced to focus on stories they don't understand or don't interest them.

There is so much value in variety—variety of content especially. Libraries offer that. A home library is something that each homeschooler builds bit by bit, but can never hold as much as public and private libraries.

When my children go to check out books, I have them get a mix of nonfiction with their fiction interests, and every once in a while, they are allowed to read a silly graphic novel like *Apocalypse Bow Wow* or *My Big Fat Zombie Goldfish*, but I make sure that my little ones know the value of word content and storylines as well. That is a main factor in homeschooling.

Another wonderful way that libraries engage children (and even toddlers and babies) is through children's story hours. These free programs at local public libraries are held regularly. When my daughters were young, we walked to the library once a week for their Wednesday morning story time.

Each visit, the children would hang up their coats, grab a mat, and sit before the librarian. She would then take about twenty to thirty minutes to read a variety of selected picture books to the children while displaying the illustrations.

It was a great way to teach my children how to behave in a group setting. They learned to go to the bathroom before and afterward, raise their hand if they had a question, and not be disruptive to the other children. After the reading, parents could help their kids do a craft project that was set up with supplies and a theme that matched the books read that day.

Once a month, the Gift Of Reading program gave each child the ability to walk around tables full of free books and choose one to take home and keep. My daughters loved it. We made lots of friends and learned a lot from each other.

When we moved further away from the city, I found that the libraries were trying too hard (for my tastes) to incorporate new technologies into every facet of their events. Instead of having a warm friendly librarian read to them each week and get to know them, the librarian played an eBook on a projector.

This may serve some parents and children well. Audiobooks and eBooks are useful tools for some settings; it just wasn't for us. Thankfully, because different local areas have different ways of doing things, homeschooling parents can test out story hours in the neighborhood, and if they don't find it to their tastes, they can attend neighboring county libraries. No one is standing at the door checking to make sure you live in the area to participate; if anything, they encourage people to branch out; you just can't check out books from public libraries that don't serve your area.

I took my daughters and their younger brother back to the library we liked and had a great time. Having the choice is what home education is all about, even when seeking group activities. Unfortunately, during the pandemic, libraries everywhere were shut down. That may have been the most difficult aspect for my children. Their love of going to the library to look for new books to read is something they have treasured from an early age.

Now that things have regained momentum, events and group activities have commenced once more. This is especially good news for homeschooling groups that either meet at the library or are organized within them. Library homeschooling groups are another great resource that costs little to nothing. Public libraries offer free homeschool meetings where specific group projects are planned once a month to encourage children to work together to build something, create artwork, problem solve, and more.

No matter which library we're at, my children's personalities shine through as they meet other children and work toward a common goal just as they would in a public school or a private-school setting. Some children are shy; some are outgoing. That is true regardless of the situations they are put in.

Allowing them a space to be around others helps them to learn who they are and grow their communication skills as they learn to be around other children. It is a great socialization builder for parents who fear that homeschooling will stunt their children's ability to make friends or interact with their peers.

My eldest is shy and soft-spoken. No matter how many dance classes or library events she is submerged in, that is just how she is. Her sister is completely the opposite. She walks up to every kid, introduces herself, and asks if they want to play. She's often seen in the center of a group of kids. Just as my eldest son thinks every boy he sees is his buddy. He starts up conversations with boys ages one to twelve without questioning himself, but my youngest is bashful and more like my eldest.

They are all socialized the same way, with the same methods and approaches, but they were born to be different people and our visits to the library have helped them accept and appreciate this. It helped me to stop questioning myself and homeschooling as we journeyed through each school year. Library groups that meet regularly often have returning families. This allows parents and children to grow comfortable with each other on their own terms, just as they would in a larger classroom setting. It's an enriching experience that builds friendships and leads to good connections.

There are other library events that are more sporadic. Author book signings, local author events, seasonal group activities, and more may not have a routine that draws in repeat groups, but they offer new opportunities, connections, and inspiration.

A few years ago, a colleague of mine lent my daughters the Fablehaven series. The books highly entertained them and reminded them of the Harry Potter books. My eldest enjoyed them so much, she was thrilled when she learned that the author, Brandon Mull, was coming to our city for a book signing. We stood in line and waited with a crowd of families on a school night because I knew her enthusiasm deserved support.

A love of reading isn't just fostered by finding the right books; sometimes, it grows with the anticipation of new material, or even getting to hear about the writing process from a friendly best-selling author. Everyone was invited into a big event room at our local library. The entire room was filled with chairs, but plenty of people poured in to stand at the back.

I was glad that I planned to get there early. We were able to snag front row seats and really hear what Mr. Mull had to say as he welcomed us and joked about his family and writing experiences. He then went on to answer audience questions.

It started getting late, and the room was full of school-aged children, so everyone was finally asked to line up to get their books signed. The event was completely free, but there were copies for purchase as well. The author took time to talk to everyone who came up to his table, one by one, and took pictures with fans.

This may seem pretty standard, but I've been to book events where authors charge for pictures or one-on-one time. The fact that this was offered to us through the public library system was truly a gift we cherished. My daughter still talks about it to this day because when it was her turn to get her book signed, he seemed very perceptive of her shy nature and straight up asked, "Are you are a writer?"

My daughter loves making up her own little stories. She nodded and blushed. Moments like that melt teachers' hearts. It gave my daughter confidence as well as a better understanding of the publishing industry from a new perspective.

Libraries across the country host these kinds of events all the time. They were delayed or canceled during the pandemic, but many open states have already resumed these wonderful teaching resources, and hopefully, others will follow as we move on.

Similar local writer events are often hosted by libraries, public and private. Children's writing contests and groups meet in library rooms and explore their creative side. Local author book signings or workshops help give children the tools they need to communicate with the written word, even if they're just looking to improve their essay skills or learn about journalism and the structure of writing articles.

Even if a child doesn't want to grow up to be a writer or a journalist, these skills improve their abilities and help them find value in computer skills. Most writers draft their work online nowadays, but even those who longhand must have their work typed up to send it off to editors, agents, and/or publishers.

For parents living in areas with bad Internet connections or households that may still be without a computer or an Internet connection, public libraries are an essential resource for learning. Children are able to play educational games or explore educational websites, while parents can gather online materials and print off information as they see fit.

Once again, our tax dollars are paying for public libraries, whether we use them or not; parents get a better value if they utilize these facilities for their benefit and the benefit of their children. These organizations may seem similar to the public education system because they are funded through taxes and designed for public use. Some may question, "If you're using public libraries for educational aid, why not just send children to public school?"

That is a valid question. One that deserves a proper answer. Unlike public schools, public libraries are solely funded through localized taxes (32). Public libraries are still locally funded, overseen, and community-based.

Public schools were once very similarly organized, but with the creation of the United States Department of Education (33), federal standards have taken precedence over local efforts. The farther away from home oversight is, the less connected it is to the people and the specific interests of the students being served. To put it simply, families in California have a different environment, values, and culture than families in Missouri. Just as families in New York City have very little in common with families living in rural Wyoming.

There is nothing wrong with this. Our differences can be strengths if we respect and value them properly. Instead of working to cater to these different needs based on localities, federal systems, especially the federal oversight of public education, has continuously worked to streamline standards and factorize education across the nation without giving thought to the different frame of reference that comes with living in different states that have different landscapes and needs.

Public libraries, on the other hand, operate with all of this in mind. Because they are still locally funded and controlled, they better serve their areas and the people who reside in them. Every library has book request forms where readers can ask for certain titles to be acquired and shared. This gives parents and children direct control over the material, which allows minorities the ability to receive books that better represent them, even if they're not initially on the shelves.

There is better supply and demand, understanding, and growth without federal red tape slowing down the process. This also makes budgeting easier and audits more accurate, thus providing a healthier learning space that offers a broader variety for students.

Those students then feel more welcome and accepted. They are more likely to want to participate in special events like Pajama Story Time or come to see puppet shows. The summer reading club was always a huge draw when I was a child. My children have carried on this tradition, and although it has been modernized to fit the technological age, being rewarded for reading is another great tool that aids home educators in fostering a life-long love of reading, which promotes learning, self-awareness, and appreciation of others.

Most of the special events at public libraries are free, but even the ones that charge admission are usually low-cost and just designed to cover extra expenses or liabilities. Sometimes, the World Bird Sanctuary does a presentation at our library, or police officers bring in K-9 units to familiarize children with their role so they're not afraid of these multispecific public servants.

Minimal fees for these kinds of experiences are well worth it to homeschooling parents. The affordable cost is returned tenfold, as our young students learn the meaning of having good values, respect, and the ability to care for all types of creatures.

Best of all, accepting support from families relieves some of the pressure placed on homeschooling parents. We work hard. We get tired. Some days, our lessons just don't get through—same as any teacher—and we have to change things up in order to drive our points home.

Signing up for the occasional library event or making story time a regular aspect of the homeschooling process is a perfect element for balance. We can sit back and allow someone else to take the lead or be the focus for a while. No matter how much we plan and prepare and budget, we all have our bad days. We may not be able to schedule them, but we can offer the occasional surprise library trip at our discretion. That is something that public school teachers are likely not often afforded, at least at the grade-school and middle-school levels.

Instead of wracking our brains and crying over a tight budget, we can rely on the "free" resources at public libraries (that we've already paid for) and find ease as the school year flies by. I cannot say enough about the value of libraries and how they aid homeschooling families, especially those of us who are living on a budget.

If fiscal concerns are the only thing holding you back from homeschooling, or you're already teaching your children and having a hard time, please spend more time at your local library and sign up for their events. Check out a couple of private libraries, and look into free book programs like the Gift of Reading or Dolly Parton's Imagination Library (34) to slowly build your own home library and fill it with both fiction and nonfiction titles that serve you best.

There is a world of books out there, and an entire universe of online materials to be read, discussed, and shared. Public schools and private schools all have their own libraries, they also encourage students to take advantage of finding books at public libraries. Most of these schools have their own computers, tablets, and internet access for students, but those that do not, again, support the exploration of public libraries because of the benefits these wonderful facilities offer.

Homeschoolers in the modern era have just as many options as private and public schools. Whether this is common knowledge or not, it's a simple fact. Free resources are everywhere. Most are just waiting to be found in public libraries.

Even private libraries and home libraries serve as pillars of homeschooling. They prop students up no matter what their family income level is. And best of all, they keep everyone connected.

Staying connected in the modern age is a huge deal. Even when the world shut down, we were able to keep learning and communicating thanks to the World Wide Web. Libraries have known the value of this powerful tool for decades now. They offer free Internet access and computer time to the public, but as coding and technology careers boom, it's important for homeschoolers to have their own computers and/ or tablets to sufficiently teach their children, which leads me to the next subject: Internet teaching tools. The next chapter is all about online learning websites, classes, and even schools.

Again, families with little to no access to the Internet can use public libraries to stay current with the times. They provide a nice stop gap for anyone who is looking into homeschooling but still unsure, but eventually having a computer at home and proper Internet will offer the best education possible. And that has always been my main goal. I know I can teach my children and provide them with the best education possible, so why shouldn't I?

The argument over whether or not the Internet should be considered a public utility has been fought again and again. Though I do prefer to implement classic teaching methods, I also see the value in also teaching modern ones as well. Some parents facilitate their children's lessons completely online; others prefer raw materials like workbooks and experiments. I find that a mixture of the two offers the perfect balance in my home, and so the Internet is a valued resource that has been a part of my teaching process from day one.

Library computer time softened me up to the fact that online games can be fun and educational. Limiting screen time has always been one of my major concerns. I am a hands-on person who prefers the outdoors, but that's why boundaries and testing the waters through public libraries can help home educators to find their way as they enter their journey as teachers and scholars working to impart knowledge and wisdom to the next generation of thinkers. Our resources fill the rooms of our house of learning; they are the proverbial furniture, so to speak.

THE POWER OF THE WORLD WIDE WEB

The Internet changed homeschooling forever. Instead of having to search through libraries and bookstores for guides and material, parents nowadays can find a plethora of information waiting to grace computer screens.

This took a long time to build up. The old adage "You can't believe everything you read on the Internet" is still true, but there are countless valuable resources both online and offline that help students type up work, explore their skills, and research various topics. Over the past few decades, the World Wide Web went from being a virtual Wild West to developing into its own networks of communication and information-sharing.

From fiction to nonfiction, satire to trolls, the amount of websites, articles, essays, posts, and more has increased to such a degree that modern home educators face the opposite problems of their predecessors. Instead of having trouble finding teaching materials, homeschooling parents now have so much information to sift through, they have to decipher what sources are best and which are just the usual Internet gossip. Many home educators rely on some kind of Internet aids. We research, test, and come to trust certain sites and programs while also disregarding sources that do not properly educate or instill the sort of values that our curriculums host.

The proper term for this is media literacy. It's not enough to know how to read. Parents must have or develop the ability to scrutinize what each website and webpage displays.

With so many news sources and varying philosophies on everything from education to pandemic protocols and censorship, it can be overwhelming at times. Information overload is real, but if you're already paying for a home Internet plan and debating homeschooling or looking to expand your homeschooling techniques, the World Wide Web is a place to cut costs while still wielding the proper knowledge to impart.

I count myself as lucky, or blessed (to me it's all the same). I started homeschooling from the start of my children's educational careers, so I was able to learn and grow with my eldest. Not every parent has that luxury, and I understand that, but because I am a chronological thinker, I'm going to first discuss websites and online practices I utilize for my younger children and then detail the more mature content.

I have a few great teachers in my family. My ex-husband's sister is an early-childhood education teacher who loves what she does and works within the public school system. I respect what she does and expressed that to her when discussing my family's decision to homeschool.

There was plenty of talk about concerns regarding socialization and proper teaching methods, but after a bit of understanding, she suggested I look into the *Starfall* website. I had never heard of it before, but it was a favorite tool in her school that engaged young children and got them excited about learning to type and use a computer while also enhancing English and math skills.

My own Internet searches for good children's learning websites were littered with online homeschooling universities that charged way too much and websites that just didn't suit what I was trying to do, so I went home that night and pulled up *Starfall.com*.

It was bright and colorful. It was diverse but in an organic way. It was not preachy or political, and it was full of classic nursery rhymes, classical music, and content that just made me smile. I sat my eldest in my lap on the couch and propped the laptop up on the armrest. She automatically took to it. The free features had little cartons to help learn to read and pronounce all of the letters of the alphabet and count and identify numbers.

That was enough for us at first, but as my daughter began to excel, I looked into the paid plan. This opened up more pre-school features like colors and shapes, as well as math games, books, and other reading aids that went up to third grade. The fee was a mere $35 a year and $30 to renew annually.

After a few months of enjoying the content, my daughter learned her ABCs forward and backward and even started to read on her own—she was three years old, mind you. This led me to sign up for the full plan. The small fee was well worth the value. I've paid it every year since, keeping this website a core element of my children's early education.

Each child favors different features. They all have the subjects they prefer. I was shocked to learn that public schools started veering away from this wonderful tool in favor of *YouTube* videos. Harry Kindergarten was suggested to me when my youngest daughter, and second child, started her pre-school lessons at home. This rapping kid had nothing on *Starfall.*

It wasn't for us. I'm a little more old-fashioned. I like starting small and simple and then expanding from there. It seems that nursery rhymes and classic stories are being left behind in the public education system to power ahead into the future without looking back.

How each parent schedules their children's learning has varying factors. Technology is a great way to connect with others and move children forward, but I think we need a balance as well. When the Internet goes down, my kids still have plenty of materials. Modernity is part of their process but not the only focus.

From what I know, apparently, a lot of new teachers, especially early-childhood education teachers, want to be the cool modern influence in their students' lives. In my niece's public-school kindergarten class, instead of learning from great websites like *starfall.com*, she was introduced to a rapping teacher duo who tried to teach math by rhyming about licking your friend when you eat ice cream.

If *YouTube* videos engage your children, don't be afraid to use them, but in my time homeschooling, I've learned that even teachers perpetuate passing fads. Some parents love the Cocomelon videos. The Baby Shark phenomenon was everywhere and inescapable for those of us who just didn't get it, for a time. Even that song "What Does the Fox Say?" was fun for some homeschooling parents because pop culture can be a different way to connect your children to the outside world even when homeschooling does not.

These little songs and videos can offer positive or negative influences depending on how they are implemented into your curriculum, but they are free, and the time you share with your little students is what matters most. I'm not a fan of Big Tech and its political influence, so I limit *YouTube* videos, but both of my sons love Parry Grip's music and we found that on *YouTube*. There will always be little compromises to make.

Thankfully, websites like *Starfall* continue to excel and educate. Their lessons now go up to fifth-grade reading and math. Also, another website my children have frequented is *PBSKids.org*. The Public Broadcasting Service (35) has been around for a long time. It was established in 1970 before I was born. I grew up with it.

Educational programming like documentaries and children's shows were a staple in my life. Now that most everything has gone digital, the PBS children's learning website is a nice tool, but I monitor it with a closer eye because some of their material is overly political, even the children's content.

Like public schools and some public library systems, public broadcasting is, by nature, more liberal-leaning. This is a fact that does not bother me because I am conscious of it and I wish to raise my children to understand varying perspectives even if a lot of our ideals and values are now considered more conservative.

The *PBSKids.org* website has fun educational games and video clips that can benefit most children. Unfortunately, some of what is considered acceptable material for preschoolers is still not acceptable to me as a parent educator. My prime example is when I allowed my youngest daughter to watch a *Martha Speaks* video. This show was all about enhancing vocabulary, and so I thought nothing of it, but this program taught my five-year-old the definition of the word *discrimination*.

Here I was baffled. I figure children should be focused on learning about themselves and the direct world around them from their perspective first and foremost before they are faced with the painful challenges of concepts like discrimination. That is my personal opinion, and there are plenty of parents who disagree with me, and what they allow their children to be exposed to is their business, but I do not want a public TV station teaching my children about serious, complex issues like discrimination. That is my job. We often discussed how we were different from many homeschoolers because we are not affiliated with a church, and the slight Native American heritage from my maternal grandfather's side of the family, but instead of focusing on the few people who will look down on us or shun us for not worshipping their way or looking and acting a little different, I have always taught my kids about the similarities between our beliefs and lifestyles of others—that most people want the same things: good food, a place of their own to feel comfortable in, and so on.

My focus isn't even to just throw vocabulary words out there; it's always to give my children the philosophy and understanding they need to properly communicate their feelings through speech in the real world. We steer clear of *Martha Speaks* now, but games and videos featuring the Kratts brothers, Curious George, and even Nature Cat are usually very balanced. Shows and characters will come and go. My son has taken an interest in Daniel Tiger, who was originally featured on *Mr. Roger's Neighborhood*.

During the pandemic, things got tough. PBS is liberal-leaning, and so even after medical reports were released confirming that COVID-19 wasn't as deadly (36), contagious (37), or harmful (38), their games and shows encouraged children (who were never at much risk (39) if any) to wear masks and social distance.

Many people left the public education system for unscientific masking policies (40). They learned just how damaging true social isolation is (41). For PBS to support unhealthy protocols and write them into their content was quite a line in the sand for my family. Their network and website are free, but unless you agree with their politics, I always advise anyone asking for my perspective to be weary of their work, especially during questionable times.

Because *PBSKids.org* went bust on us, I had to find something better. My eldest is also growing more mature each day. She's no longer a little girl. She craves older materials. We have found a lot of success utilizing *khanacademy.org*.

Khan Academy is a free website with lessons for all ages in any subject. They are a worldwide mecca of information, which includes lectures, reading materials, skill practice, and so much more. My eldest is a math whiz, and though I got pretty good at it in college, I'm rusty. When my old math notes can't help me facilitate a proper lesson, we turn to *Khan Academy*.

The best part of this site is that parents can track their children's progress and customize lesson goals. Students are able to explore a variety of materials and learn at their own pace. My daughter likes to work first, play later. Her little sister needs more time and breaks in between. Having this flexible option is endlessly useful to us.

Again, like all content, parents need to check in on things. One reading comprehension lesson confused my daughter because an assessment question mentioned a girl having two mothers. My daughter knows about the gay community. She's not being hidden away from the world; she has a friend with two mothers, and so did I when I was growing up, but having it in her school test questions stopped her for a moment. It distracted her from the lesson because instead of focusing on the story, she had to stop and ponder this different lifestyle.

We discussed it, and I came to find that it challenged her to think more critically. She was annoyed that it stopped her from breezing through her work, but she needs to slow down sometimes. I don't believe that all school material should include all minorities all the time because they do not always represent everyone, but it's a good lesson to question ourselves, even as we teach and properly display the diversity of the world around us, so I considered the situation a teachable moment.

How we perceive outside material is per our discretion. As my eldest grows into a teenager, she has earned some more freedoms online, but that is based on her interests and she is still heavily monitored because of the risks involved with online interactions.

In addition, social media has become such a common aspect of life. A lot of parents wonder when and how it should be introduced to children. Depending on the site, age requirements can range from thirteen to eighteen, but the only social media I consider a valuable, socially acceptable resource for minors is *Goodreads*. *Goodreads* allows older middle-grade and young-adult readers to explore books, track what they've read, and connect to other readers.

It doesn't have the constant stream of posts yet allows users to express their opinions on books or join groups discussing their favorite genres. There is a lot a young student can learn from this, with the proper guidance and monitoring.

I consider *Goodreads* a simple opportunity to introduce a balanced example of social media, and even similar to learning apps because it is less about interacting with others, and more about tracking progress, growth, and interests.

For parents who prefer tablets and cell phones to laptops and computers, learning apps are in abundance. The *Goodreads* app is very accessible, as is the *Starfall* app, for example. My children have enjoyed playing some other learning games, especially to practice their multiplication tables and fractions, but there are so many popping up each year that it is hard to keep track. There are also concerns about how addictive apps can be. Like a lot of screen time engagements, online resources are great tools, many are free or affordable, but for homeschooling parents like me (who wish for our children to value real-life experiences as much as their training with technological advances), boundaries and ground rules must be set, followed, and enforced.

Locks or parental controls make this super easy. There is a definite need, and so these features give home educators the ability to set specific timers, limits, and cut-offs for when we are not able to immediately shut off devices if our children get carried away.

Again, this is all at the parent's discretion. Plenty of us test the waters and decide what works and what doesn't. It's less costly than investing an entire year's worth of curriculum into something that just isn't working for you and/or your child.

Online resources are abundant but do pose a lot of outside influence. A good rule is to assume that when a student is online, they are essentially walking down the proverbial Internet street and can be exposed to as many outside influences, if not more, than when they leave the house. Teaching children to be safe and cautious of any messages or pop-ups that may break through security systems is a must.

Just as my parents taught me not to give our personal information to strangers when I was a kid, I teach my children that when we leave the house *and* when checking their emails and learning online. If they see or experience anything questionable, they are to report it to me and my husband right away. One of us is usually nearby if not watching, so it's not a big deal when they're little, but as students mature and grow more independent, they won't require as much help, and so homeschoolers need to check up on them frequently.

Email, unlike social media, is more private. To encourage children to learn to type and get excited about communicating and telling stories, I open email accounts for each of my children when they turn five years old. To some parents, this seems too soon; to others, it's delayed.

I chose this age because we start pre-school at three years old. By five years of age, they are in first grade and really learning to read. Typing letters to family members helps them identify and spell words. It gets them excited about school. They can't wait to see if Grandma wrote back or if their Grandpa emailed them.

Some email services have age requirements; some do not. I found success with Outlook for my children so far, and enjoy emailing my daughters when they are away with my ex-husband.

Other providers, like *Google*, are sometimes a necessary evil. Again, I'm not a big fan of monopolies or Big Tech influencers, but Google Docs is free to Gmail users. It's universally used across schools, universities, publications, and so on. The features are user-friendly, and the main benefit is that writers can share their work without having to attach or download it because it is saved in the drive and can be shared without having to attach links, depending on how the creator (student or author) marks the security level.

Document programs are essential for students to type reports/essays and write creatively if they wish to easily share their writing with the most current universal technologies available. Microsoft Word is the old standard that is still in competition, but this is a pay-for service that needs updates and has changed a lot with the times.

For parent educators and students who wish to support smaller word processors that are not tech giants, Scrivener and other independent document generators offer expected formatting options and lessons that walk new users through their writing steps and features. Some are free or offer tiered levels, but most offer pay-for add-on packages based on specific needs.

In addition, typing tutorials and even coding websites for children are growing in demand and popularity. The *Typing Club* is a perfect example of a free online resource that helps slowly teach good typing skills and finger placement. This website offers lessons for children in left or right-handed comfort, as well as Dvorak keyboard training (which works off of a different keyboard layout).

As homeschooled students type better, they may become interested in coding. Coding is a growing field and just fun for expanding math and computer skills, and it's never too early to offer children new puzzles. My youngest daughter has a blast playing on *Kodable.com*, and my eldest found plenty of coding content on the *Khan Academy* website to keep her interest.

Having these broad tools to teach expanding subjects is something homeschoolers of the past have never had. Our children are accessing ideas and theories that were only dreamt up within the past few generations. It can seem fast and confusing at times, but that's why breaking them down from early education levels on is less intimidating and more inspiring.

Nearly every learning website requires a login account to be created. Associating emails and passwords are common. As a teacher, my information is what I utilize to manage these accounts, but as my eldest grows, I do anticipate that she will eventually switch over to facilitating the ownership of some of her accounts as she earns her independence and proves her ability to self-govern.

Every home educator has to make that decision based on what is best for their situation. After all, that's why we're taking the reins and leading scholarly pursuits.

Free and affordable websites and email options are teaching tools that any child can enjoy. If spam or junk mail shows up, parents can use that opportunity to slowly introduce their children to simple media literacy concepts like limiting information to trusted sources and choosing to use their time wisely. As I usually tell it, "You only have so much time to read. You could read all day, every day, and you would never come close to reading all the books and articles that are out there, so make sure what you read is worthwhile."

These philosophies will carry children through adolescence into adulthood, and we need to make them aware and literate of the media they will most likely encounter online. Introducing news articles and filtering research resources is another skill homeschooled students can perfect online.

Wikipedia is easily updated or edited by non-certified sources, so I never trust the site, and have taught my children to be weary of it, But *Britannica.com* and other credible sources that are backed and funded by unbiased—or at least highly experienced and educated—individuals and/or organizations have better, more trustworthy information. As media bias and public school politics infused during the pandemic, a need for raw, honest, educational material is being sought each day. Parents who are fed up with the dividing principles of newer ideological radicalization are funding and supporting fun educational resources that re-engage children in learning, instead of preaching at them about what they should believe. From Ron Paul's homeschooling curriculum to *PragerU Kid's* content, there is a balance to the challenges presented by modern-day social deconstruction.

Trusted reports, essays, and media links are difficult to find nowadays. Having dipped my toes into journalism during the pandemic, I can say that I lost most of what little faith I had in journalistic integrity.

Not to be grim, but mainstream news sources shocked me as they ran sensationalized pieces that promoted fear and panic, instead of offering truly factual scientific understanding. Yet, even when I gained freelance positions with independent media sources that claimed to maintain "unbiased" political ideologies or conservative stances, the main goal was to get more clicks. More reads, shares, and comments were always the focus. I didn't write stories because I wanted to get rich; I tried to impart knowledge or shine a light on the truth. Unfortunately, that doesn't always sell, and even when it does, it often upsets the powers that be. When some of my articles were too honest, I was punished or distanced. It was a constant battle that led me to walk away.

The point is that parents have to be prepared for discussions about the nature of media and how it can propagandize. Also, we must be as educational as possible without discouraging hope or purpose in the next generation.

Taking the time to find journalists, essayists, authors, and publications that you trust is a necessity. Especially for parents teaching older children. They need the flexibility to question themselves and their teachers (you)— with respectful debate and discourse—while also understanding that one news source or one book is never enough to base an entire thesis on. The more sources, the easier it is to logically determine the common facts and find the truth hidden underneath all the money, politics, rhetoric, and bias. Many media sources are funded and controlled by singular figures, so using multiple sources that are run from the same root is also not advised.

This is work. It's tiring. It can be frustrating. Both students and parents can, and likely will, experience information overload at times.

Free and affordable online resources are of value, but so is time off. Having nature days or no-tech time is something we implement in my house to remind us all of what's really important. The Internet can become divisive, even a battleground of sorts. It's good to log off and go take a walk and see your neighbors smiling at you. It's helpful to pull out workbooks and dust off classic print stories to keep students connected to the physical world.

Balancing an understanding of the Internet and free online resources with real-world material is another great lesson for teachers and students alike. The Internet can lend life more color and paint the interior of our internal schoolhouse, but we cannot forget the windows to the world: our hands-on lessons. So let's move on to chapter five and let in some fresh air.

PHYSICAL MATERIALS: BOOKS, WORKBOOKS, AND KITS

O ur true windows to the outside world come in various shapes and sizes. The Internet seems like a great way to connect but often offers a parody or edited replica of true-life experiences, so although online learning resources are a great help when educating children in-house, physical materials also have a big role to play in a well-rounded education.

These range from hard copies of physical books to workbooks to craft kids to hands-on project materials. Each of these various items engages a different learning style and hosts a variety of activities that teach children to enjoy the learning process as much as they enjoy other activities.

Books are a given. E-readers and online stories are great educational tools, but there is something about holding a book and turning the pages that encourages children to look at the world around them with fresh eyes. Parents witness this every time a baby or toddler picks up a board book and slaps it. As they learn to turn pages for themselves and point at pictures, they also tap letters and words with their fingers, and supplying children with material doesn't have to empty your wallet. Used book stores are everywhere. Even resale clothing stores for children usually have used books for sale at a fraction of the cost that big corporations charge for new books.

This makes it easier to establish home libraries with materials you wish to pass on for years and years. Reading time is sacred in our house. It is a core element of my children's education because learning to read helps them develop the ability to study independently and explore topics on their own as they age and mature. Just sitting and reading to young children while following the words with your finger gifts children the understanding that the words on the page are the most important aspect of the book. Without those printed letters, the story would be incomplete. Wanting to hear the story and learn what happens excites them; it leads them to ask questions and allows their curiosity to help them find the answers to develop their understanding of the world and define themselves and their place within it. Bargain book stores and book sales make finding these materials much easier for homeschoolers. Half Price Books in the Midwest is a life-saver sometimes because they carry a wide selection that small resale bookshops don't always have. Making sure my children have what they need while staying within budget isn't impossible thanks to stores like this.

It is my belief that what a child reads determines the kind of education they will receive, not just that they know how to read and have access to books. The quality and storylines matter as much, if not more, to my family and me. Nonfiction is a genre that isn't as highly sought out but highly important for a proper education, and I consistently seek it out for my children.

Finding quality non-fiction books, and even textbooks as the children get older, is a must. Thankfully, many public schools, public libraries, and even private schools generally host annual book sales where they sell their older books and textbooks for a small price. It's important for homeschoolers to seek these events out in order to find the best value with the most current information. Nonfiction moves fast and is being updated every day, especially in the science fields, so we have to be on the lookout for a good deal every day. It doesn't hurt to be friendly with neighbors whose children are in public school, or private schools, and to check ads and community event sections of papers and online resources.

From the day we decide to take control of our children's education, we have to accept the full responsibility. It sounds like a lot of work, and it is in theory, but truthfully, once you find what works for you, the pressure eases and there are great moments of value and relaxation as your children excel and trust you as not just a parent but also a teacher.

Starting from the beginning of a child's educational career lays a wonderful foundation that forms a solid bond right away. I read out loud to all my babies before they were born. They came into this world knowing my voice and my love of passing on information. This instilled a deeper connection to reading and led them to love their books and just listening to others from such an early age that they adore storytelling; print, or campfire tales.

The oral tradition of memorizing stories is another great lesson homeschooling parents can pass on. The best spoken-word tales that my kids beg to hear again and again are true stories from my childhood, or stories my grandfather told me. They adore learning about how "Mom did this" or "Grandpa did that."

Just because these stories are not printed in a book does not mean they cannot teach others. If anything, teaching from your experiences is a homeschooling trick that gives many students a leg-up on those who have only known public school regiments and strict curriculums. These stories are free. The memories that last are there for a reason, and passing them on is a unique teaching tool that parents can share with pride, a strong sense of culture, faith, and values, for the bargain of just spending some time together.

This approach also helps me focus on nonfiction so I *can* get my kids interested in books about historical figures who may seem too far removed from our modern lifestyles to be interesting. The more I connect my children to the past, the more they wish to learn about the different people who came before them—and not just in our country but from areas all around the globe.

Nonfiction helps us paint a better picture of history lessons than just memorizing dates of battles and the names of generals. It lets us learn about cultures we never knew about and customs that are different and exciting.

Even board books for babies are printed with nonfiction stories and tales of true life, so these lessons don't have to be held back until a certain age. It's all up to parents when and how they wish to teach about all the wonderful real-life people, places, and things that exist and came before us. Parent educators can really give their children a realistic sense of self by choosing stories that teach values as well as early science and math concepts like identifying animals, insects, opposites, and the concepts of shape and size.

As children begin to recognize sight words or even sound out stories to blossom into independent readers, it's important to offer a wide variety of cold books. These are books they have never read or seen, and so have not memorized. This is a perfect way to encourage them to keep expanding their knowledge while also testing to see how their reading skills are developing.

Book blocks, which are small board books that come in a nice box with a window-type door and a handle on top, are wonderful for early and pre-readers because they have simple stories and about 6 pages. Each of my children had their own book block set to carry with them for outdoor lessons on nice days, and even for use as potty-training aids to keep their attention while learning to use the bathroom.

From there, the I Can Read books, and Step Into Reading series offer wonderful ability-based aids that parents can introduce to children and use as they increase their reading abilities and comprehension. There are plenty of options, topics, and genre varieties in both of these helpful book series.

The first book my eldest read was from the Berenstain Bears' I Can Read Box Set. Her younger sister did better with the Step Into Reading books. My eldest son is plowing through more classic books, like the Dr. Seuss I Can Read Books. *Go Dog Go*, and *Hop On Pop* were important influences when I learned to read, and my son has latched on to those style of books as well.

Classic books seem to hold more weight with my children. Maybe this is because I have nostalgia for them, but sharing what you love with your kids is a big part of educating them to love learning. Even if you don't enjoy reading, sharing at least one story that you appreciated in your youth will pass that spark of interest onto your child(ren). Because my mother held onto the books my sister and I grew up with, we have the special gift of being able to pass many of our favorites down. Keeping your books for your children, or their books for their children is another way to pass on knowledge for free.

There is also the added benefit of seeing the excitement children display when you give them your favorite book and tell them that it is now theirs and that you are trusting them with a special volume that you held in your hands when you were their age. That generational bond is something we can all relate to and cherish without paying anything.

This might be partly why I prefer classic books. It may also be that modern books sometimes concern me because they seem more focused on pushing political ideologies than gifting children the ability to think for themselves. Sure, Dr. Seuss's works took on political narratives, but they still told a story to help children look at specific situations from a personal standpoint.

Having written a few children's books myself, I prefer to share books that teach universal ideals. Material that kids connect to is usually hopeful, uplifting, or funny. Kids love to laugh. They need to feel as if they matter and they can make a difference in the world. Even when taking on challenging subjects, it is important to let them be heroes instead of victims. Heroes can grow up and make an impact, whereas victims lack confidence and have perpetual excuses that drag them down.

Teaching confidence is something homeschoolers seem to have down. Minority parents are better able to uplift their children with "black girl magic" or pride in their heritage, while the majority can welcome everyone without checking boxes and expecting everyone to act the same way.

Eric Carle, Don Freeman, and Doris Burns are classic authors with picture books that speak to my children with a great sense of wonder. Roald Dahl's children's chapter books present some of the best sympathetic characters with hilarious moments, just like Beverly Cleary's The Mouse and the Motorcycle books, the Harry Potter series, and anything written by Francis Hodgeson Burnett. The Anne of Green Gable series and Little

House on the Prairie books are staples for my daughters as well, but so are nonfiction stories like *The Diary of Anne Frank, Freedom Train*, and the Who Was? children's biography series that detail the lives of individual historical figures from various ages, races, and cultures.

The freedom of physical homeschooling materials doesn't start and stop with books. They are simply a favored aid because of storytelling's links to our histories. Reading is a special ability because readers have so many options to choose from, and once they get going, they can truly study for themselves all throughout their lives.

Once children get going, it's hard to stop them. That can be both inspiring and terrifying at times, but that is parenting in a nutshell. One minute you're taking off the training wheels, propping your children up, and the next they're coasting downhill looking ahead while you applaud them from behind.

I find this a regular occurrence when it comes to workbook studies. Pre-school and kindergarten workbooks aren't hard to find. They offer fun activities like coloring alphabet letters or tracing numbers and finding where they're hidden in cute pictures.

This is where I truly found peace in homeschooling. Helping my children trace shapes and learn their colors by simply breaking out the markers and coloring a picture by number or helping my children learn to do simple dot to dots gave both of us the confidence to have fun with homeschooling lessons. We always start at the same time each morning and do the workbook lessons first, so we can do crafts, outdoor time, and experiments in the afternoon.

They may seem a bit outdated, but workbooks offer some structure when our lessons veer off course. Putting pen to paper is a physical activity that better connects students to their work and the world around them. From pre-school to middle school, there are a lot of workbook options to choose from. This is where costs and budgeting really get tested as students grow older.

A simple pre-school book is fun for young children. They can sit for about fifteen minutes and have fun filling out a page. The School Zone's

Big Preschool book has everything a young child needs to practice in it. Their worksheets are fun and engaging and filled with great lessons. My children used them until about first or second grade when the need for more challenging material grew essential.

One of my main goals is to keep my children on track without blowing our entire budget on sub-par materials. My eldest enjoyed some of the Brain Quest flashcards, but when we tried their workbooks, they seemed a little behind, as if they're more geared toward prepping children for going into the grade level marked on their work.

Then, I found the Comprehensive Curriculum Of Basic Skills workbooks. These massive publications are filled with over five hundred pages of learning material. They range from pre-school through sixth grade and are closely aligned with standard education requirements. When we first started using them, they were advertised as approved by the Department of Education. I'm not sure if they lost that approval or what happened, but the content is still as educational as ever and my children have enjoyed them so far.

Once my eldest crossed over into middle-school territory, she took to the Spectrum Workbooks with ease. Unlike the other brands, these are split up by subjects, so they take a little more funding and planning, but they offer a wide range of language arts, math, and science books. In testing these out on my youngest daughter, I found that she doesn't enjoy them as much, so we'll have to find something else or power through. Finding trusted resources is a priceless aspect of homeschooling and making sure to offer the best information possible is key.

Beyond that lined paper, cursive workbooks and even Sticker Stories are also handy. My children love to write and draw, so having enough paper in the house is nearly impossible, but we stock it as needed and teach the children to conserve paper. They have to fill both sides and focus on making sure to utilize the entire page.

Then, with Penguin Random House's Sticker Stories my kids get the added benefit of finishing a book. Instead of just creating another picture to hang on the refrigerator, these wonderful sticker books tell a tale. They are laid out for children to decorate the illustrations with stickers. Once we complete ours, they are treasured storybooks that we read again and again. Some are nonfiction scenes that depict animals or vehicles; others are fantasy stories that feature mermaids or unicorns. My only complaint about these little books is that there aren't enough of them, but there is so much more to homeschooling than just reading and workbooks.

What really makes the homeschooling experiences are the hands-on learning moments. Doing experiments, crafts, and nature projects is something I wish we had done more when I was in school. A lot of activities and projects can easily be put together using materials that are already in parents' homes. Other materials and supplies aren't often very outrageous.

I like to keep things simple. If I find a link to a science experiment that has fifty pieces and twenty steps, I wonder if my children will relate to it, or get frustrated trying to get everything working. The Kidz Labs science kits are well worth the cost. These usually come with everything a child needs to perform a specific experiment, especially instructions that help parent teachers get their bearings on how to help. These helpful kits start for children twelve months old and go up through fifteen years.

Over the years, we have used the 4M Kidz Labs kits to explore bubble science, witness our own volcanic eruption, learn about magnetic science, build our own robots, mine for crystals, and more. The kids really love these experiments because they get to conduct them themselves, and seeing how different things react to each other gets them excited about learning how the world works.

The variety also appeases all the different tastes and interests a single roof can contain. My eldest is a girly-girl, so she likes crystal science and crystal mining; my youngest girl is more into seeing how things work and watching cool patterns, so she prefers to set up water rockets and build the solar system. My three-year-old son is *obsessed* with robots; he somehow got it in his mind that he needs to grow up to be a robot programmer so the robots will be nice to people (I may or may not have mentioned that once; just once and he latched on). The Robotix kits are pretty fun.

Like erector sets and other building toys, they teach children to apply the basic principles of math and science directly. These kinds of activities display cause and effect while making learning fun and interesting.

Because actions speak much louder than words, I'm more likely to get through to my kids by lecturing them while we do experiments or even have craft time. They listen better when their hands are busy. Implementing crafts into school time is one of the greatest elements of homeschooling. It is more engaging, and finishing a project offers a sense of accomplishment that all students need, especially as the years go by.

State requirements are often very strict on core classes, so it is vital that parents keep track of the time, but art class is something all children benefit from and it gives home educators a break from the heavier subjects that require concentration and serious thinking. Now that my eldest is nearing high school, her art projects do take a lot of work. She likes to sew and knit, but her dedication to them is a valuable reminder that someday she will be in charge of herself and so she has to have a good work ethic.

Unlike science projects—which are often done within the span of an hour or two, depending on the subject—crafts take more time and patience. Even my son has to wait for his paintings to dry. Learning how to wait patiently is another free teaching tool that comes with homeschooling.

I may have to budget for construction paper, glue, yarn, and other materials; these can always be acquired during a sale, and the lessons my children draw from what we make last as they grow older.

Making up our own crafts is something I've enjoyed. Reusing or recycling old bottles to turn into sculptures, transforming oatmeal containers into drums, and painting boxes into little houses not only helps teach my children to be resourceful and utilize the things around them in different ways; it also instills the value of conservation and being conscious of our own waste. Plus, there's the added bonus that they will design their own crafts.

That's not always feasible. Sometimes, a teacher needs a little help. So, if you're more of a kit person (like I am with the science experiments), there are three main brands of children's craft kits that I have used for years and trust from both the parental and educational standpoint.

I'm always looking for a deal—more bang for my buck—and to purchase as many useful education materials as possible to round out a good school year. Because of this, I've tried a lot of random brands and supplies, but my children and I have found the best successes with ALEX brand craft kits, Creativity for Kids options, and Melissa and Doug Created by Me!/Decorate-Your-Own crafts.

The ALEX and ALEX Jr. craft kits have been a staple in our home since my eldest was a toddler. They have crafts that range from toddler ages through grade school. Although my girls have outgrown them a bit, they love to help their little brothers with their kits, or sometimes still do the simpler projects just to have something easy to do in-between more rigorous studies. Each kit is low-cost and comes with more than enough to offer children the option to follow an art project yet still make it their own.

Creativity for Kids is another trusted brand that offers a variety of educational kits for small fees, but this brand is not as focused on crafts alone. They offer up lots of mini gardening kits that come with seeds and dirt and a container all ready to go. We've gotten more Grown N' Glow Terrariums than our kids can care for, and there are also functional crafting options like kits that guide children to make their own night light or water globe.

Our favorite project is the 3 Little Books kit that comes with three bound and blank books and a little book holder. It comes with stickers and markers for children to write and illustrate their very own stories. Children who feel as if they have a voice are more likely to appreciate reading and writing because it shares their thoughts and ideas. This special project instills that.

My eldest, who is a bit ahead, finished hers during her kindergarten curriculum after she turned five years old. Her sister, who struggles more, completed hers at the end of her first-grade year when she was six years old. I have no idea if my son will want to do them next year or in three. As a parent educator, I get to evaluate their progress and determine when they are ready instead of letting federal agencies, public schools, or age numbers on boxes determine what is best for my kids, and that makes all the difference.

These sorts of projects are also a nice change from the ALEX crafts that generally just get hung on the wall for a while or put in art portfolios. Instead, my children tend their gardens, play with the sewing creations my daughters make, read their little stories to each other, or enjoy a little light when they go to bed and worry in the dark.

The value lasts through many grades, and I realized that even though I went to public school during my childhood, my mother spent plenty of money on craft crats through the years. Plenty of parents do regardless of whether or not they are homeschooling, so home educators get the added benefit of implementing them into their teaching process instead of having them run into other family time. What we spend on these engaging supplies is saved through the lessons and the sense of self-worth that is grown, while also allowing more time for other events and activities instead of having to find the time to work these moments into our schedules.

I, of course, couldn't mention crafts and kits without bringing up the ever-popular Melissa and Doug brand. Not only do they have some of the best puzzles, large and small (the floor puzzles are so exciting for young children), but their craft kits are more decorative and functional as well.

These also make great birthday presents, so when family and friends ask what my children want for their birthdays, craft kits are a simple request that offers flexibility and lightens our spending load. We also enjoy giving them to others because kids like doing things. They enjoy working with their hands and feeling the rewards of finishing something themselves. My children's desire to share that joy tells me that we're on the right track, or at least veering toward it.

Every parent has to assess their budget and their child's interests, but having these options expands the possibilities of homeschool learning experiences, and I've saved the best option for last. Many children learn best through real-world physical lessons. It's not enough to read or do a worksheet or paint a picture of a butterfly; in order to fully grasp the world around them, they must study other creatures.

Maybe it's because I'm a biology fan or because my children love animals (like many do), but whatever the reason, our favorite affordable learning resource is the living projects found at the Nature Gift Store. These easily supply parents with everything they need to help their children care for caterpillars and observe them as they turn into butterflies and enjoy the wonders of helping tadpoles grow into frogs. They offer ant farm kits, worm farm kits, Venus fly traps, and even hermit crab starter kits.

This wonderful business has clear instructions and packages for parents to humanly transport and facilitate science projects that include living creatures. They take careful time and planning. Children need to be educated on not just life cycles but also the needs of each animal to keep them alive and thriving.

My children have enjoyed these lessons so much that we repeat them. My son loves the Caterpillar to Butterfly kit. Because they need warmer climates for a successful transformation, this is best done in late spring, if not over the summer.

The first time we tried this out, the butterflies all emerged around my son's birthday and so he felt as if they were a gift. I had ordered two kits so we could do an additional experiment. The rules say not to open the caterpillar cup when they arrive in the mail. This is a good policy to have because anything could happen to the caterpillars if released, but because my children have been raised gently holding caterpillars, and have even had butterflies land on them, we opened one of our two cups. I allowed the children to hold the cute little insects for a short period during an afternoon class. Then, we put them back in, safely.

Thankfully every caterpillar was healthy. They all made their chrysalides and emerged new and ready to fly. We released them outside once they all broke free. Parents also get the added benefit of knowing that they're helping these great pollinators. They're wonderful for flower beds and tend to stick around.

The tadpole-hatching kit is a bit more involved. These little guys need more space and have to be properly fed. My youngest daughter loves frogs, so our first try was full of excitement and plenty of reading about frog development.

It was so exciting to see their legs grow and their tails shrink. My husband and I were also enamored. I must admit, one of the tadpoles died about halfway through. Whether it was overfed or just ailing, we don't know, but that was another important lesson for the children. In biology, we must accept the fact that even just studying an animal can be heartbreaking. For parents of faith, this is a time to allow religious understanding to shine on science.

Home educators can choose to embed broader life lessons into these fun-loving science experiments as they see fit. And in truth, parents who don't wish to pay for a kit can go out and catch caterpillars or tadpoles with their children. That is exactly what I did in the early teaching days to sometimes cut costs, but I found that in gathering supplies it is actually much cheaper to just grab a kit, and the animals involved have a higher rate of survival when coming from a specialized nature store.

As homeschooling grows in popularity, so does access to helpful teaching tools. The need for affordable materials and project resources is being supplied by demand. Parents are resourceful and ingenuitive. If we don't find the right reading materials, workbooks, and hands-on learning kits, we will create our own. Thankfully, there are so many options nowadays, that parents should be able to find what their children need without going to too much trouble or having to spend their entire paychecks.

Best of all, we have outside resources that can offer aid when homeschooling needs a little boost. Our physical materials are great, but field trips, summer camps, and community programs are other resources that parents can budget for, which often have low-cost options for those who shop around.

We may enrich our gardens and the exterior of our homes with all the great hands-on resources mentioned in this chapter, but getting out in the community is what paints the homeschooling house with a rainbow of love and experience.

FIELD TRIPS, SPORTS & ART PROGRAMS, AND SUMMER CAMP

That big scary word *socialization* looms over homeschooling parents. We're all subjected to unfair stereotypes. Plenty of people imagine that all homeschoolers shelter their children or try to drill religious texts into them, but nothing is more frustrating than the false idea that homeschooled children are all socially anxious and unable to interact with others. Being taught at home *is* a different educational experience, yes, and making sure that children get out and explore the community is a necessity, but in the modern era, it's really not a big deal at all. So, how do home educators ensure that their children find group activities and play with others outside the house without spending thousands of dollars?

The answer doesn't take a college degree. It's closer to home than we think. All over the country, in every state, city, and even the next neighboring county, public parks, museums, historical sites, zoos, and more are just waiting to be explored.

Public parks are some of my family's favorite places because they're already paid for (by our taxes), so we own them and care for them. So do the other families that frequent these areas.

Between the span of my childhood and that of my children, many people have put playgrounds and trampolines in their backyards. It seems like a great idea. Why not keep your children entertained? But an unfortunate side-effect of everyone owning their own playground is that children—yes, even public-school and private-school children—don't get out and meet the neighborhood kids like they used to. Everyone lives in their own sectioned-off worlds.

It seems more expensive to me to run around buying large pieces of equipment for personal use when a park playground literally sits just a mile down the street. It seems much more costly to pay for the insurance hike caused by owning a trampoline, even if parents buy one on sale. Maybe I'm old-fashioned or just more extroverted, but I'd rather make use of the free services available to my children, especially being that these encourage my little ones to get out and make new friends.

Parents don't have to pick one over the other. It's possible to have a backyard swing set and still take your kids to the park. I just find that most people (at least in my area) don't. They use their personal recreation equipment as a way to entertain children without having to be as involved.

It's during our walks to the park that my children and I play counting games and go over multiplication tables. It's during the free play time at public parks that my sons learn to interact with others and follow the rules of games like tag and hide-n-seek. They also learn the value of freedom. They are being raised with the freedom to race other boys while my daughters swing with new friends.

Public parks are also a great place for children to mingle with varying ages without boundaries or constraints. In real-life situations, people aren't segregated by age and generation. The best lessons I even learned as a child came from listening to older kids warn me about certain things. I also earned a greater understanding when passing on information to younger kids who showed an interest in my favorite subjects.

So, contrary to mainstream rhetoric, parents *can* socialize their kids without sending them off to public school, and better yet, they can socialize them without spending their entire budget on one single field trip. What's more, there are plenty of free options depending on what places they're exploring.

Public parks are great for picnics or field days. We frequent them in our off-time. The best free field trips I've found are hikes through nature reserves and historical sites.

Depending on your area, access may be questionable, but every homeschooling parent should search their city and state park databases for these treasured places. In my home state of Missouri, we have many great nature reserves. One of my favorites is Lone Elk Park (42).

This wildlife management area is full of bison herds, elk, wild turkey, deer, and more. Visitors can drive through, or stop at specific picnic shelters.

This land once served as an ammunition testing and storage area during WWII. It was called the Tyson Valley Powder Plant, but after the war, it was turned into a park. So, not only does this place offer animal observation in a natural environment but also historical value. Because it means so much to me personally, despite the fact that it is free, there is a donation box at the entrance, and my family always drops in a few bucks. That's how we pay homage to most of these sorts of places. If everyone gives a dollar, the preservation of the area is ensured regardless of how taxpayer money may be spent.

Rockwoods Reservation (43) is another important close-to-home site because it is one of the oldest conservation areas in the country. This 1,880-acre reserve was decimated by limestone mining, but eventually, people realized how badly this practice affected the environment and so it was turned into a protected area in 1938. Now, it thrives with towering trees, wild grasses, and an abundance of animal life.

Places like these give children a stronger sense of history and reality. They appreciate the land they inhabit and are just as eager to learn from the past as adults are. All across the country, places like this exist. They are often free or charge a minimal sum for parking or entrance passes.

Nature reserves gift us the ability to connect with our past with a more presentable lesson. They are a true bargain that we've already paid for through taxes and life lessons, so it's kind of silly not to take advantage of them. Plan a visit.

Like these great resources, historical sites are also perfect for low-cost field trips. Just a simple Internet search for "historical sites" followed by your city or county will produce a variety of new options. Parents can call ahead and schedule guided tours or show up during public hours. Some historical sites do charge admission; some do not. It often depends on the location and restoration maintenance.

My husband and I have taken our children to mostly free historical landmarks—places like Cahokia Mounds (44), Zumwalt's Fort (45), and the Daniel Boone Home (46). Sometimes we splurge for a hybrid—sites where it's free to go to the landmark but costs to get into the museum. Guided tours are an added expense that is sometimes worth it but can easily be cut out when things are tight.

Either way, these trips break away from routines when lessons grow mundane. They re-engage children throughout the school year, bring dry history lessons to life, and get kids excited about the people and cultures that came before us. Best of all, a lot of these historic landmarks have museums that offer child-friendly play. Even at the Lincoln Presidential Library (47), there are hands-on learning experiences where children can walk through miniature replicas of Lincoln's childhood home and play with educational toys.

When certain places charge admission, it is often worth it, but there are so many free museums in the United States that there are plenty of articles listing the best free museums (48), and even an organization called Museums for All (49), which offers a website search function for users to find free or reduced-rate museums for families receiving SNAP benefits. Whoever said homeschooling is for "rich people" didn't do much homework.

Being close to St. Louis, my family is able to frequent the free art museum (50). My children love going there. They each have a favorite painting that we have to go and see every time, and when we go during special events, the museum sometimes offers free crafts and other activities. Special touring exhibits are easily accessible for a fee, but the museum has so much to it on its own that my kids are happy to just enjoy the usual exhibitions.

It doesn't matter how much we do or don't spend; so long as we engage the children in new activities and support their interests, they continue wanting to learn more. Because of this, my husband and I try to always budget in an annual trip to either the Magic House (51)—a super fun children's museum near our area—or the Children's Museum of Green Bay, Wisconsin, when we travel north to see my in-laws (52).

The children are always eager to go, and it's become a favored tradition. Children's museums are everywhere now. When I took the children to visit my old high school best friend in Iowa, we went to their Family Museum (53). It is a treasured memory and they always ask, "When can we go back?"

Knowing that these places get them excited about learning makes it all the more worthwhile. Budgeting for a once-a-year trip to a museum geared for children is valuable for all parents but especially homeschoolers because it does offer that extra socialization element.

No matter where we go, the kids are happy to find new friends and talk about their favorite subjects. Having these interactions can add up fast so, to cut costs, we sometimes bring a lunch and eat in a nearby park. Food and drink expenses are a slippery slope. It's easy to think, "Oh we'll just grab something cheap," but families with multiple kids better afford these events by coming prepared with their own snacks, meals, and drink bottles.

Even if places don't allow outside provisions, packing a cooler takes a lot of pressure off of the wallet. This allows parents to have more fun with the kids as they run and play while learning about science, math, and history while playing with others in a social setting.

This is also a useful tactic when taking trips to the zoo and animal sanctuaries. Making sure to come prepared and cut a few corners offers a lot more leeway. So do group packages or discount passes that lump certain attractions together. The Saint Louis Zoo (54) is one of the best free zoos in the country. It hosts a wide variety of animals that are housed in habitats, which are designed to be as similar to each creature's natural home as possible.

Although admission is free, many of the children's activities cost money except during the first hour, so us "early risers" take advantage of that. When enjoying the free hour is not possible, there is a discount pass that can be purchased at a better rate for all the activities.

Each of my children likes different animals, so exploring the zoo is an all-day event full of excitement and wonder. They're eager to learn about them. Because children tend to appreciate animals, these specific sorts of field trips are engaging, educational, and not too costly. Especially since we've learned the value of packing a backpack with extra clothes, hats, sunblock, sunglasses, wet wipes (which can come in handy even if you don't have young children anymore), band aids/a first aid kit, and even a plastic bag or two for putting trash into or holding clothes in case of an accident or spill.

Being prepared makes every outing more effective, and there's no one more prepared than a homeschooling parent. When packing a few extras, you can keep your budget on track and have fun teaching.

Animal sanctuaries are another great place to explore new animals and subjects. There are numerous wolf sanctuaries across the nation. In Missouri, we have the Endangered Wolf Center (55). They specialize in helping the Mexican wolf population recover, and though they *do* charge admission, every dollar contributes to saving endangered species.

In a nearby area sits the World Bird Sanctuary (56). Welcoming visitors free of charge, this 305-acre territory has walking trails, enclosures that house injured birds that are being rehabilitated for re-release back into the wild, and some resident birds that have been too injured to survive in the wild. Places like this have a different atmosphere than zoos. They are more intimate and personal. It is a truly more enriching educational experience.

These kinds of animal sanctuaries are more common than a lot of parents know. Best of all, they're eager for visitors to come and engage in activities. Animal-sanctuary employees are all about teaching others about the creatures they look after. They're happy to offer tours and group events for minimal fees, if any.

Fieldtrip options are everywhere. If kids aren't really interested in animals or have allergies or parents just can't commit to trips like these, even some bowling alleys, gymnastics centers, and other indoor children's activities host homeschool days where they openly invite homeschooled children to come and enjoy their facilities. These are a great introduction to another wonderful educational tool that home educators should look into: community programs.

Some kids are more active than others. My youngest daughter and eldest son need extra physical activities to help get their energy out. Community sports programs are vital for them to set goals, focus, and learn teamwork.

My eldest is calmer and more interested in domestic endeavors. Art classes serve her better because she can quietly learn new skills and creative techniques.

No matter what interests a child, looking into sports programs and/or art classes enriches the homeschooling experience with an outside perspective on the world through extracurricular exploration and skills. It may seem like an odd topic when discussing low-cost home education, but if you shop around you can find programs for a nominal fee.

Community centers are best. Corporate chains may have big names, but they set pricing at a national standard, whereas a local rec-plex is better suited to each area's cost of living. Thankfully, there are always exceptions, of course.

The YMCA (57) has a great track record for community-based, low-cost youth programs and assistance for underprivileged children across the nation. This is mainly because they are an organization, not a corporation. Their program fees are the lowest my family has seen. My daughter has done both basketball and volleyball at the Y, and teamwork is encouraged with parental involvement. Parents are asked to volunteer as needed. When short-staffed, the YMCA asks parents or other family members to step in and take on the role of coach or assistant coach.

The first time I coached, I didn't know what to expect. It was a learning experience for all of us. As I became more seasoned, the value of getting to have those extra hands-on moments solidified my appreciation of being a teacher and leading young children through life lessons.

Community centers and recreational facilities offer fun sports programs that can be competitive but are centered on fun and learning to work with others—and they're not just limited to sports clubs. Their art programs offer quieter, more thoughtful practices. These are a perfect socialization primer where students can come together while receiving instruction from a teacher other than their parents.

Like the sports programs, they are often affordable, but instead of hosting competitions and sports-based groupwork, these are structured around more individualized activities with all the supplies children need. Many places even host art exhibits or display cases with students' artwork, so they can be proud and look at what others have been working on as well.

The frequency and variety of these extra activities offer home educators the flexibility to properly shape our schedules. Some kids are more social than others. Some need more structure and guidance. Sometimes, community activities are a hit; others fall flat.

When my daughters were younger, they were regularly enrolled, but now that they're older, sometimes they ask for a break, or my husband and I need more downtime to let everyone just be home together for a while without having to worry about rushing off anywhere. Like everything, it's a balance—one you will find as you go—and it changes and shifts through the years as your kid's interests change and they grow more knowledgeable.

The last and most optional out-of-home learning experience for homeschoolers is summer camp. Homeschooled children crave friendship more. They value one-on-one connections to a higher degree than other kids. They may not statistically have as many friends as public school children, but the bonds they forge dig deeper, and they need that, so giving children the opportunity to form lasting relationships with other kids is something I specifically value as a mother.

Children who are shy and cling to at-home studies need more understanding than others. Two of my kids are extroverts. They're friends with everyone and always ready to go out and talk about their favorite subjects. The other two are bashful, shy, much more reserved, and always concerned about what others think.

These are common personality traits. Even when immersed in the most social settings from an early age for long periods of time, some children develop into introverts, and others do not. Instead of treating "socialization" as some kind of lifestyle outcome, children respond best when they are allowed to explore interactions with others at their own pace.

My extroverts are into sports and art. They want to join as many community programs as possible. Because of this, summer camps offer the variety they desire without unloading the budget.

Now, I'm not talking about expensive overnight camps that used to be all the rage for rich people seeking to plop their children somewhere safe so they can travel to Europe alone. That isn't feasible for home educators living on a tight budget. In my experience, day camps are much more cost-effective and allow students a proper range of social time along with periods at home afterward to digest all they've experienced.

Day camps can range from just a few hours on a single pre-determined day, to a week-long daily drop-off camp, or even a six-week summer session of play and activities. Each option is priced based on time, materials, and so on. Of course, shorter day-camps generally cost less and so they are perfect for parents who are just getting started.

The length of the camps usually follows the age of the children enrolled. Preschoolers have a harder time being away from their parents, so it makes sense that single-day camps exist for them to just play and have fun with other children for a small 3–4-hour block. The fees for these kinds of programs are minuscule, and the experiences they have last for ages. Scheduling a single-day activity also allows more flexibility for tight schedules.

Most kids, even my shy ones have so much fun at short single-day camps, that they ask for longer ones, so it's no surprise that the most common summer camps my family has found and taken advantage of are the single week day camps. For these affordable programs, children are dropped off each day, during the span of one week, and picked up in the afternoon/evenings before dinnertime. These range from half-day to full-day camps, and again, the length often depends on age ranges.

When my eldest danced for St. Louis Ballet, she enjoyed Ballerina Princess Camp. This was a great resource where she spent under four hours at the studio each day (for a week), twirling in tutus, learning about ballet, and doing ballet-related crafts with other girls her age.

She was wholly committed to ballet for nine years, and throughout that time, she did longer camps. Then, her interests shifted during the pandemic, and she became more passionate about horses. Horseback riding is an expensive sport—one my family cannot afford to enroll her in throughout the school year—but we have found a nice middle-ground with a local farm that offers week-long day-camp programs at a reasonable rate. In addition, there is a ranch that offers one-shot trail rides, which can be scheduled during any time of the year.

These outlets give families the ability to explore something that they cannot afford as a regular expense. It's a nice compromise. Parents have the option to add it as an annual event that kids can look forward to all year. Families that just don't have the income to pay for monthly sessions and ongoing leagues find comfort in community summer camps. They provide a sense of freedom to combat a bad monetary flow and prevent low income or economic uncertainty to hinder every aspect of life.

They're also helpful for children who aren't as focused on one subject or activity. My youngest daughter likes so many different activities that a simple rec-plex day camp better suits her because each day has something new to offer. She doesn't have to like just dancing or learning about one kind of animal.

When I was a kid, we didn't have much. I was only able to go to a day camp one year just before I turned six, but I still remember it: the laughter, making friends, being outside in the summer sun singing together, and making crafts.

Then, through the Girl Scouts program, my parents were able to send me to a week-long overnight camp just before I entered middle school. Again, they only did this once, because we were low-income, but the experience has lasted a lifetime. Knowing that some kids never get these kinds of experiences makes it even more important for me to budget them for my children and donate to programs that help others do the same.

Not every child needs to go to camp. There is plenty of fun to be had in a backyard or on an apartment playground. Even so, just one summer camp experience can uplift a child's desire to learn.

For parents who think this is a waste of money or that they just can't afford it, I urge you to do some online searching. Call around. Most YMCAs and community centers offer discounted rates for members. Looking into just how cost-effective this is benefits each family as they work to navigate through the various programs and options. All children deserve a well-rounded education, and part of offering that is stretching your dollar to provide them with experiences that teach life skills and how to be independent.

Thankfully, if times are really tough, the Boys & Girls Clubs of America (58) offer low-cost or even free activities for children living in poverty. It's easy to find a local club and get involved. So no, summer camps are *not* just for rich people who have money to "throw away."

And like I mentioned in the context of my own childhood, scouting programs also offer low-cost summer camp events that will be remembered for a lifetime. Overnight camps are something I have yet to pay for, for my kids. They are much more expensive than day camps, and I'm a greedy mother; I want as much time with my children as I can get.

Whether they go in the future will be based on many factors. Mainly cost, educational need, and if my children wish to go.

For now, I see day camps as a happy medium—a way to remind myself to let go and step back as my children grow older. Because my eldest is shy, she has no interest in going away for a week. Her sister and my eldest son (as extroverts) are a different story. They're already asking about it, and so I've already started shopping around and making budget assessments.

If they do go to some sleepaway camp, I'm sure it will be a mixture of nervous worries and blissful relaxation. Until then, day camps are our best available option. Campers bring their own lunches, hats, sunglasses, sunblock, and so on, which keeps the fees down since they don't have to provide food, dining areas, or sleeping quarters. There is also less liability for everyone all around, and that always lowers costs.

Whether sending a child to summer camp, enrolling them in a community art or sports club, or just taking them out for a fun field trip, these social outings make the educational process more fun and exciting.

They keep kids engaged in seeking new subjects to instigate that passion for learning that drives a person to keep seeking knowledge and wisdom through various tools and methods.

Not to sound too cat-postery or like some inspirational commercial but I fully believe in the power of introducing our children to different teachers and subjects even though we are homeschoolers. We can't always be there for them; no matter how hard we try, there will come a day when we are gone. Whether that will be when we're lying on a Florida beach retired or in spirit, we must prepare our kids to handle the world even when we're gone.

Enrolling children in summer camp and various community events helps them learn to handle themselves and find their own place in society. Being present for them during field trips allows us to still come along for the ride sometimes but in a setting that displays how many other people there are to connect with and just how much there is to experience in life. It builds confidence and self-reliance; two major characteristics that our children need to grow into successful, healthy, happy adults.

Socialization cannot be imposed. It doesn't naturally occur when factorized or forced, but scheduling trips and outside courses definitely benefits homeschooling children and gives them the opportunity to get out with other people without costing more than parents can pay.

These experiences are arguably more valuable that the most up-to-date textbooks, websites, and reports. They may seem scary at first, but the longer a parent homeschools, the more they realize what a gift it truly is to be an educator in any setting. My children ask questions and openly discuss what they know.

When I was a child, my view of education was very different. The last thing I wanted to do was talk or even think about school from the moment I got off the bus to the second that I had to go back the next day. Even if I had a good day, school and home were separate. My studies were something that belonged in the classroom. My mom would ask me the ever-pressing question, "How was school?" and I would shrug, or answer, "Stuff."

Instead of following that meandering path to knowledge, my children cannot stop talking about all the things they know and wish to know. It's an ongoing discussion that comes up at any time of day, or anywhere we go. This catches on quickly. When we're at the zoo, other kids open up to my children about their interests. That spark of excitement lights up their eyes. *That* is what homeschooling is all about, and *that* is what makes our budget worthwhile.

Those moments can be drawn out more frequently. There are more ways to find a community within the community—one that brings homeschoolers together and allows them to share in their strengths and improve their weaknesses. What am I talking about?

You'll have to turn the page to get all the details because this is the topic of the next chapter, but it entails a bit of insight into the entire world of homeschooling. It is especially helpful to parents whose family and/ or friends do not support homeschooling, but it's nonetheless welcoming to those who are just starting out and looking for a bit of guidance. This is a wonderful way for home educators to share techniques and bring their children together within the community in a group setting designed specifically for homeschooling families: co-ops.

Community-operated homeschooling groups are like little mini schools taught and led by parents who are teaching their children themselves. They are just one more resource that parents can use to homeschool on a budget, and they truly make a house feel like a home.

HOMESCHOOLING GROUPS

Homeschooling groups may seem intimidating at first. They're usually already established, so if you're new to them, you will be able to get to know everyone and how they work along with your children. It may take a little getting used to, but these groups exist to specifically offer a stronger sense of community by helping homeschoolers reach out to one another on a regular basis for support and educational sharing.

Home educators know that leading by example is the best way to teach, so even if parents aren't extroverts, they must seek social events in order to help their children gain the full benefits of their schooling experience. Some parents wait until they've been homeschooling for a while to test this out, and others dive right in.

I spent so much time focusing on my children in the beginning that it was years before my family finally joined a co-op. Part of my apprehension was that I was already fighting to prove to friends and family that homeschooling was our best option. It was so exhausting, I just didn't have the energy to reach out. It seems silly now knowing how much support we could have had, so I urge parents to get in contact with these groups, *especially* if you're not receiving the proper support of extended family members and close friends.

The first step to this is, of course, finding a group. So how does one do that?

Like all collective activities, groups form in different ways. Some come together within communities and are relaxed; others are built with structure and organization. Neither one is better than the other, but I was hesitant for years. I felt like my daughters' dance and sports activities were enough.

Then, when all of that shut down during the pandemic, I realized that literal pay-to-play groups aren't there for you when the world faces unprecedented stress. I found a laid-back homeschooling playgroup on Facebook that was meeting at a public park. This was after the initial shock of the pandemic wore off and the data showed that the virus was not the plague faulty algorithms predicted it to be (59). It was the fall of 2020 and my children were eager to play.

We packed up and went. Just like that. No tip-toing around. No messaging back and forth. It just felt right. As soon as we arrived, I smiled. The parents sat on the grass and talked. It was a nice social event. The kids ran around in a big group and enjoyed just being kids. That sense of normalcy meant everything to my family.

I liked going, but the group usually met in the middle of the day during the week. As a writer, everyone thinks I get to make my hours, but meeting deadlines is what pays the bills, so I can't just sit at the playground for two hours every day. A lot of the moms seemed shocked that I worked, and they laughed at the fact that my husband and I had a strict schooling schedule for our children.

Some parents take the freer approach of letting their children do their lessons whenever they want, but I find that my kids do better when they have a regular routine. We start at the same time each day and focus on specific subjects at certain times.

This is not the only way to teach; it just works better for us. If you find the more relaxed approach better suits you and your family, I support that, but after leaving the group, my kids still lacked a social outlet away from home. Most classes and groups were resuming, but a lot of them required masks, and I couldn't muzzle my children. That seemed cruel and unnecessary.

Online searches for more structured groups kept bringing up co-ops. These community-operated organizations were always in the back of my mind. Though they charged a small annual fee and required parent volunteering, my curiosity had been growing since the day I started teaching my eldest at home.

It was at this time that I was taking on some freelance journalism job, so when I got the opportunity to interview the founder of the most prominent co-op near my area (60), I jumped on it. Most co-ops have an acronym as their name. That makes it a little difficult to find them online, but they advertise on social media, in community magazines, newsletters, and on good-old-fashioned bulletin boards.

I had known about S.H.A.RE. (St. Louis Homeschooling, Activities, & Encouragement) (61) for some time, but meeting with their leader, Cathy Mullins, gave me the insight I needed to find a group close to home. Her eyes shined, and her laugh was infectious. She spoke to me like a friend, not a reporter, and I was touched by her sincerity. She really believes in education freedom and the power of involved parents. Her personal homeschooling journey is one of struggle and triumph in caring for her sons and losing her youngest, so I felt honored to spread her message through the *Epoch Times*, with my article (62): St. Louis Homeschool Pioneer Details Her Journey Through Teaching.

Any parent who is nervous about joining a co-op or just isn't sure about homeschooling should contact a local group. While speaking with Cathy, I learned about the co-op in my area called, SHINE St. Charles (63). She highly recommended it, so I looked them up and found their website sponsored by Homeschool-life.org (64), the same site that runs hosts the S.H.A.R.E. site.

If an internet search doesn't pull up a group in your area, try adding "homeschool life" to your search keywords. This website provides a wonderful hosting service, and it's incredibly welcoming to parents who wish to form a group and create a simple website if their area is underserved.

Once you find a group or two, give yourself time to learn about them. I live in an area where there are multiple groups, but S.H.I.N.E. St. Charles is closer to home, and its mission aligns with my values. They are a Christian group that welcomes people of all faiths with their commitment to, "Education with Integrity + Virtue." Those are universal values, and they do not preach specific religious texts.

Values are a big part of finding the right group, but so is making sure your schedule works and what kind of fees are required. Checking to see if volunteer time is required and when to join is important to note as well. Our group meets on Wednesdays. My family recently joined halfway through the spring semester, which meant that most classes were already full, but it gave us a leg-up for the next school year because returning families get class-choice preference. New families do not get to register as soon as returning families because many of the returning families have parents who teach classes and are wholly committed to the cause.

So, how and when families join a group is also something to consider. To get officially connected, most co-ops just ask for some standard information: name, address, how many children will be participating, and their ages.

There's often an annual fee—which is so small it's well worth the bargain—as well as added fees for optional field trips, classes, and extra-curricular activities. Even with inflation, our costs are usually under $20, just to offer an idea for estimation.

Parents looking to join a co-op should also be open to helping out. Because these organizations are community-operated, and homeschooling is all about parental involvement, so is volunteering to help in classrooms and even teaching. The best way to figure out if this suits your needs is to shoot off an email or just call the group organizer.

I wasn't entirely sold on S.H.I.N.E. St. Charles until I spoke with the director, Sheila. She was so friendly and welcoming that all my apprehension dissolved. That's the great thing about homeschoolers: we understand the power of direct interactions and we love to help each other.

Once a family joins a co-op, there's so much to learn. Depending on the organization there may be a variety of classes to choose from. If there's not, asking to add one is never frowned upon. I enrolled my eldest first. She's the most introverted, so I thought, *If we break her in, everyone else will do fine.*

I didn't know what to expect. That first day is always difficult for both parents and children. When we got to the location, we had trouble finding the right door, and it was pretty cold out, but once we entered the cafeteria, it was like stepping into any small school.

There were kids everywhere. My daughter's first class took place directly after lunch and was held in the cafeteria. It was a filler class called "Socialization through Board Games."

It seemed perfect. I imagined kids playing Monopoly in a quiet setting. Even homeschoolers sometimes fall for homeschooler stereotypes.

The group was playing card games, telling jokes, and constantly being asked to quiet down. It was a bit of a shock to my soft-spoken daughter, but so was public school for my shy older sister. Like everything, she just needed to get used to it to warm up to others. Afterward, she *did* need some time alone but agreed to keep going. We both knew that she needed to be around other kids her own age without her younger siblings constantly distracting her all the time.

She struggled for a bit, to the point that I even bribed her. I told her I would get her some chocolate after class if she actively participated and really tried to get to know everyone. This incentive made it a hundred times easier for her to smile and interact with other kids.

I'm usually pretty health conscious, and not a fan of bribery as a common parenting or teaching tactic, but she needed the boost and I found it was worth it. She's settled in now and our weekly co-op experiences just keep growing.

My younger daughter took to the group much more easily. She walked in and took a look around at first. I was worried that I had failed as a parent and my kids really were socially stunted by homeschooling, but she quickly proved me wrong. As soon as she got a feel for the place, she found some kids to talk to and was soon laughing and playing.

Co-ops make these situations more intimate. Classes are smaller. Ours allows no more than ten children per class, so everyone really gets to know each other. Because the classes are parent-led it's easier to be friendly and reach out to each other.

These once-a-week school experiences give home education those added experiences that help students prepare for college, jobs, and life in general as they age, but they're not all that co-ops offer. For a minimal fee, field trips are also available, but they're never required, and students are not expected to attend.

Instead of having to worry about permission slips and attendance, co-op field-trips are held on a different day than classes and operate more like a group of friends getting together to experience something new. There's less pressure, less tension, and no worries about who sits with who on the bus because parents drive the students and come with them. We get to learn with our children instead of just leaving it up to the teachers, and in exchange for a few dollars, we bond with our children on a deeper level than other parents. That involvement matters to them, even if they don't always admit it at first. You can't put a price tag on showing up.

Plus, some field trips offer new perspectives that lead to a fountain of questions. S.H.I.N.E. St. Charles does an annual tour of The Missouri State Penitentiary (65). It may sound strange, taking children to go see an old prison, but this place has a lot of history. Although it shut down for use in 2004, it has been used since 1836, so going there gives students a lot to think about. Parents too.

They also do a homeschool activity at the Foundry Art Centre (66), tour the aforementioned Daniel Boon Home, and other outings. Homeschool co-ops are known for organizing great field trips, so being affiliated with one broadens horizons and offers more possibilities for exploring places you might not have even known exist.

Just having the option is nice. If things are tight, we skip the trips, and having that flexibility is one of the most relaxing benefits of joining a co-op as a home educator. The freedom to come to a single one-hour class or spend the entire co-op day at the facility is also freeing. It operates more like college, where students get to make their own schedules and take the number of classes that suits them.

Best of all, there are more benefits, and some of them don't cost a penny. Some parents worry about their children missing out on things like holiday parties, school plays, dances, and graduation ceremonies. Co-ops are where that gap is not only filled; it's fulfilled with enriching opportunities to be a part of those celebrations and more.

They are like mini private schools. They often rent out church basements or community center rooms, so they have the space to host plenty of childhood events. The one I most appreciate is picture day.

It may be silly and clichéd, but I'm a mom and I want pictures of my kids as they grow—especially nice clean professional-looking ones. Our co-op has a picture day each semester, but instead of pressuring families to purchase expensive packages like schools did when I was a kid (a tradition they've carried on to this day), parents pay a minimal price—a donation of the parent's choice at our group—for a flash drive of the images.

This is so much simpler. People who have a photo printer at home can just do it themselves, and those of us who like matte photos or borders and enhancements can go through whichever photo printing service they choose. It saves money, and best of all, parents can just email digital copies or share them with friends and family online. It's less stressful than having to cut out one-hundred wallets and throw them at everyone during the next family reunion.

School photos, like many other events, are accepted as normal aspects of growing up. Thanks to co-ops, homeschooled children don't just experience this but also school parties, plays, and dances. Throughout the year, community-operated home educating schools can throw Halloween, Christmas, Thanksgiving, Valentine's, and other parties. Whatever the parents choose to recognize can be introduced.

At S.H.I.N.E. St. Charles, they celebrate all the holidays and even have an end-of-year picnic. These special get-togethers are sometimes held during the lunch hour; some are after classes on the regular Wednesday meet-ups.

As more and more schools remove fun parties like these to avoid offending anyone on religious or cultural grounds, co-ops work to better fulfill the needs of children and parents to happily celebrate their faith, cultures, and more. I was in public school when the fight to remove

Halloween raged on. Some overly-religious parents claimed that Halloween was "evil." When they tried to ban it across the board, everyone was upset and so the compromise was to host "Fall Harvest" parties.

I don't know where the idea that Halloween is "evil" came from. The holiday itself stems from the same type of customs as Los Dios De Los Muertos and All Saints Day. Its Pagan roots literally trace back to a holiday to honor the dead. Remembering those we've lost is something all people of all faiths have done for ages. There's nothing wrong with that to most people, but because a select few were upset, public schools re-branded them and banned certain fun elements.

Banning something that offers all children and families a community experience for the sake of a few is exactly why public schools are failing. Instead of working with everyone to mediate and uphold American customs and traditions that promote national pride, public schools seem to be taking away more and more programs to implement policies and events that are less connecting.

Just as Halloween is cultural and exciting for students, Christmas came up on the chopping block next when I was in school. Whether I celebrate Christmas or not (as an adult), I understand the need for children to celebrate the season.

Not all Christians incorporate Santa Claus into their traditions, and even my former Jewish employer used to decorate a Hanukah tree. There are plenty of creative ways to allow everyone to exercise their right to religious freedom without banning this or demonizing that, and homeschoolers are so creative that we work to focus on throwing fun parties for the kids instead of arguing over politics that honestly do nothing to serve the community.

Best of all, these special events are homegrown, so moms and dads can bring decorations and make tasty dishes instead of being asked to fork over extra money for supplies. It is a balanced effort that allows parents to be involved at the level they can afford. This approach is what once made school so enriching. Somewhere along the way, everything became standardized. To get away from factorized learning, co-ops give homeschooling parents an alternative that also offers extracurricular activities like drama, orchestra, choir, and more.

The interest of the students takes precedence over everything. That means each semester changes based on need. There has to be a need for a drama club or an orchestra in order for the co-op to form them, so the opportunities will vary and change with the students. Our organization once had a full orchestra; as interest waned when the older students graduated, the music teacher remained on for private lessons and is prepared to reassemble an orchestra again if and when enough students enroll to perform together.

This grassroots approach saves money because funds are directed on an as-needed basis. Best of all, children aren't locked into something they don't wish to continue for a full school year. If they try something out and it doesn't suit them, they only have a few months before the semester changeover.

It's more efficient and conducive to a healthy learning environment. Children who are allowed some control over their schedules and involvement grow more independent. They often display better maturity and empathy.

Those who wish to expand that ability to see things from another's eyes and show an interest in acting onstage are able to perform plays, musicals, or even ballets. Some events are closed to the public, but ours are often open, so anyone can come to watch the children find the spotlight. For our group, admission is free. This element is priceless for my family of six.

Being able to take the entire family to a free show to watch their friends and peers is one of the most valuable aspects of being a part of a co-op. Homeschoolers tend to have larger families because we are more dedicated to those generational ties, and free events aren't easy to come by. Even though my children have expressed no desire to act in a play, getting to be part of the audience is something they love. It's a shared experience where they can just be part of a group and be entertained by their peers.

Now, despite being more likely to have larger families and come together for more group activities, parents with children enrolled in co-ops *do* understand the need for individuality. We quickly learn that each child needs to find their own way. Sometimes, that means taking a class with other students their age, and sometimes that means going to a middle-school dance, homecoming, or prom.

Prom is an American tradition. It's played up in movies and comes with a heavy price tag in public schools. My prom tickets were $50 each. That was twenty years ago. Then, there were the shoes, hair, and makeup to worry about. Boys had to rent a tux and maybe even buy a corsage.

Instead of decorating the school gym to host prom, many public schools now rent out hotels or banquet spaces. This seems a bit extravagant for teenagers (who are happy just hanging out in the kitchen). I've heard mothers in my area talking about buying dresses that cost hundreds of dollars and ticket prices that are well over double what they cost when I was in school, if not triple.

Yes, schooling experiences should be celebrated, but they don't need to become the main purpose. Parents are better at budgeting for parties than school administrators. We're the ones who have to make ends meet, so we know all the good life-hacks and discount stores.

Homeschool co-ops host middle-school mixers, homecoming, and prom dances without expecting families to shell out hundreds of dollars for one child's experience. They're smaller and more localized, so there's no need for renting out hotels. Parent chaperones are better at watching out for dangerous behavior to keep the party clean and age-appropriate.

These events usually cost between $10 and $35 per person—depending on your area and co-op leaders. This is a much more reasonable price tag, and still just as memorable of an event. It's like stepping back into the 1950s but with more appreciation for everyone.

Then, when the year is over, the students who are graduating get to take part in their own special graduation ceremonies. Again, these don't cost as much as public schools charge for the event. Co-ops shop around for good-quality, low-cost caps and gowns. They know where to find the bargains and how to throw a party without asking for unreasonable funding.

No one knows how to throw a party like a proud mama. No one sets up a better scene than a supportive father.

Whether receiving a diploma from an online school, getting their GED, or other high-school equivalency, students who have completed their homeschooling journey are invited to walk together and celebrate their achievements just like students at any other school. Some co-ops make this a closed, private event. Some open it up to any homeschooling families that have a child who is entering adulthood and finished their at-home learning.

S.H.I.N.E. St. Charles welcomes everyone because the other prominent organization in our area does not, and they want to offer options for all homeschoolers, even if joining the co-op isn't for everyone. This is a nice way for families who just don't see the need to join (and those that cannot) to still give their homeschooled children that big finish that is so highly publicized everywhere.

Offering low-cost graduation ceremonies to homeschooling families is a service that really displays what co-ops are all about. They want parent teachers to succeed. They're there to offer support and maybe a little guidance from others who know what it's like to teach at home.

This is always driven by the fact that co-ops are built and led by homeschooling parents. Parents who wish to impart their knowledge can easily offer a class for co-op students. The process is easier than one might think.

After just a few weeks of joining S.H.I.N.E. St. Charles, I knew I wanted to teach. I've always loved facilitating lessons. My children enjoy learning, and though I chalk that up to childhood wonder, I know that my positive approach to teaching is part of their success. Applying this to a small classroom setting—without the pressure of a Department of Education and all their red tape restricting my ability to get through to my students—is like a dream.

It's truly give-and-take. Families who have enrolled children in homeschooling co-op classes receive the benefits of their students being given the opportunity to learn from new teachers and gaining outside lessons while offering their own contributions. Sometimes, this is as simple as volunteering as a teacher's aide or on a smaller scale, but when the timing is right, certain parents are compelled to provide their own class.

Being a writer, I love English. The written word is a timeless communication tool. I noticed that many parent educators in the co-op prefer to focus their talents on the younger children. Toddlers and lower elementary students are a lot of fun. They're more excited to learn and energetic, for sure.

When it came time to propose the next school year's co-op classes, I chose to focus on the older students. It seems that there is more of a need for that. This will vary depending on the group, but in general, a lot of parents have no issues teaching their own kids as they age, yet when faced with imparting knowledge to other people's children, they lack the confidence needed to trust in what they know and are less likely to teach a class.

It's a strange side-effect of home education, but being that teaching for one's co-op sometimes saves money on other classes and expands the spectrum of teaching tools, it is an option that not only helps parents who are homeschooling on a budget save money but also practice time efficiency and test out new teaching practices.

I volunteered to teach creative writing to upper elementary students, ages eight years old to eleven years old. I also proposed an essay-writing class for middle school students in the co-op. Then, lastly, I offered to teach high school journalism.

These are all areas our group was lacking that are valuable to students regardless of which fields of study and careers they wish to pursue. I have so much experience in all these areas that I know I don't need a teaching degree or certificate to be able to conduct successful classes.

All teachers deserve respect. Anyone who commands a classroom and keeps children on track has their work cut out for them, but for too long, parents have been sold the emotionally and culturally expensive ideology that only teachers with extensive college studies and training can pass on knowledge to others, even young children. This philosophy is destructive, misleading, and just completely inaccurate.

If anything, the opposite is quite true. The best teachers I've met are the ones who use life experiences and explorative practices in order to expand minds. Without free-thinking, unconventional educators, I would never have been able to succeed. Knowing this, the value of jumping in and offering what I can costs me literally nothing while offering many gains within my own field and community.

The rewards of teaching are never-ending. They perpetuate long after you step out of the classroom. Anyone who thinks they might be able to offer something useful to co-op classes should step up and see where it takes them.

Whether teaching is an option or a curious desire or not, homeschooling co-ops are well worth the time, effort, and small fees included in membership and participation. Some families will benefit from joining for a single class once a week; others will thrive from a full day of community-led studies.

It's worth at least checking out a public event or discussing the prospect with children to gain their opinion on what's best for everyone involved. Co-ops provide the kind of support that parents can't possibly imagine as they embark on their homeschooling journey. I highly recommend them.

Even so, there are other community-driven organizations that offer support and information for anyone seeking to learn more about homeschooling or continue to teach to the best of their ability without shelling out a large chunk of their income. Co-ops are the heart of community-led teaching guides, but right alongside them are homeschooling conventions, and that's where we're headed next.

HOMESCHOOLING CONVENTIONS

When parents first start homeschooling, support makes all the difference. Having a place to go where other homeschooling families are gathering and encouraging each other really opens up the world of teaching your own children. For parents seeking direction, information, or just discounted teaching materials, homeschooling conventions provide a place for families to go and find everything they need and more.

Typically held annually, conventions offer a broad range of vendors, workshops, speakers, and special events specifically for homeschooling families. One of the most well-known homeschooling events, the Great Homeschool Convention (66), tours throughout the United States and sets up at various venues for a weekend at each location. Tickets are pretty reasonable. From individual rates to family passes that allow parents children and grandparents without a set limit, down to free shop options for the first night, this event specifically allows everyone to pick and choose which options work best for their situation.

There are plenty of other conventions, some local or within certain states, but most provide the same welcoming atmosphere surrounded by a love of education and sharing information. When first walking into a homeschooling convention, the general feel is relaxing and fun. There are booths with vendors just waiting to share their books, art supplies, learning toys, curriculum styles, lessons, and more. The variety is pure joy, and the costs all vary.

The books are my favorite aspect. The first things I see are the books. They might as well be dancing on the portable shelves, calling out, "Look at me!"

They come in different forms. During the last convention we attended, I could smell the used-book booth from the front door (I mean that as a compliment). It was the first thing my family noticed. We are booklovers all the way down to my youngest, so we—of course—rushed upon it eager to find something unexpected.

Most homeschoolers share this appreciation of reading and books. It was clearly no mistake that this booth was placed in the hall for everyone to see before they even go into the main event. No matter which convention, once homeschoolers enter the main area, there come across plenty of authors waiting to discuss their work. Because homeschoolers come from a broad range of backgrounds and income levels, vendors are good at setting reasonable price points while offering quality materials that aren't often featured in other educational settings.

It was at the Great Homeschool Convention in St. Charles, Missouri, that I found BRAVE Books (67). I instantly recognized their children's picture book, *More Than Spots & Stripes* by The Hodgetwins. This is a story warning of the dangers of teaching identity politics in schools and how it divides children rather than uniting them.

In speaking with the BRAVE Books representative, I learned that this company specifically publishes conservative books, which explore and challenge mainstream narratives to put forth logical stories that children can easily understand and identify with. They have titles that warn of the dangers of communism, teaching true gender boundaries based on biological limitations, and why the 2nd amendment matters. These serious political issues are not easy to tackle in children's picture books, but this publisher does it with grace and courage. They know their audience. Homeschooling families are tired of teachers and schools pressing their politics on children, so offering dignified opposition is in demand.

This publisher specifically offers a subscription service for their titles that was presented at a discount rate of $3 for the first month and well under the list price after that. For parents who are not sure of monthly book subscriptions, the titles are available for individual purchase, but those discounts are something that these conventions are made for. That flexibility is exactly what homeschoolers crave, especially when browsing through the material of numerous vendors.

For families who are less focused on politics and just miss the "good old days" when books were about expanding minds instead of telling children what to believe, I met with the Senior Editor of Chicken Scratch Books (68), Kiri Jorgensen, at the latest convention in St. Charles. Her vision is quite different from BRAVE Books' political messaging. Chicken Scratch Books is committed to producing traditional middle-grade stories that are free of political persuasion and other biased messaging.

Instead of worrying about gender confusion or skin color, their books focus on telling a story that engages readers and helps encourage children's love of reading and learning. They are a perfect alternative for parents and students who are tired of ideology and preachiness being forced through every facet of mainstream and even independent reading material. This option appealed so well to me I signed up for their mailing list right away and went home and perused their website that night after the kids were in bed. Independent books can sometimes range a little higher than mainstream titles, but their price point is reasonable and on par with industry standards.

As an added bonus, this publisher offers some free writing and reading courses through their website. Parents and students looking for learning guides can take advantage of these resources, while adult authors and writers can expand their knowledge of the writing craft. This option is something that I personally love because I want my children to see me actively working to learn more even though I'm grown-up to reinforce the fact that learning never stops. Plus it's always encouraging to see others offering adults the ability to better themselves.

Lastly, there are a handful of Christian publishers who usually frequent homeschooling conventions. As many home educators know that their beliefs help to encourage a stronger sense of purpose, having access to Christian books is of interest to many faith-based homeschoolers. Publishers like Christian Focus Publications (69) and YWAM Publishing (70) stand out. They offer religious stories—some that teach about history and others that offer the values and principles of Christian beliefs.

As many authors and publishers as there are, these are just the start of all the teaching tools that homeschooling families can find at these conventions. Educational toys like those from Discovery Toys (71), box subscriptions for fun learning materials (72), and art supplies including kits from Melissa & Doug's (73) line are readily available. Making sure to engage students and truly display how fun learning can be is a common goal of most educators, and homeschoolers are especially focused on utilizing everything they can to help their children reach success. One can never have enough construction paper, paints, and glue sticks. Being able to find all of these physical materials as well as cool educational toys and even kits filled with subject-focused materials is a huge help throughout the school year.

This is all just the tip of the pencil. Most of the vendors offering materials are focused on offering their specific curriculum or lesson plans. Some organizations even provide completely free homeschooling materials.

The New Classics Study Guides (74) are free to download and easy to facilitate. Best of all, they're focused on literature units for homeschoolers. My family found a Montessori Homeschooling Resources (75) representative and entered for a chance to win a free curriculum package.

Online and physical options are seen everywhere. The American School (76), Classical Conversations (77), and Memoria Press (78) all offered different lesson approaches, among many others. Lessons on etiquette are presented to help students learn traditional manners from pre-school to high school by vendors like the Etiquette Factory (79). This organization offers many resources, including children's books, and even George Washington's title, *Rules of Civility & Decent Behavior In Company and Conversation.* I was shocked and excited to find that they even offered a dating etiquette guide.

Beyond these lesser-known curriculums, parents can even appreciate finding material for courses such as Nutrition 101 and Growing Healthy Homes (80). When my family last encountered them at the most recent convention, they offered a free guacamole recipe and a healthy activity that teaches how to grow an avocado plant. The possibilities expand our horizons as home educators as much as our children's through finding new interests.

It is overwhelmingly exciting to walk along the booths. There is so much to see, and plenty of vendors offer free materials and/or lessons, so these great events save homeschooling families hundreds of dollars. For instance, homeschoolers interested in teaching their children Spanish have been offered a free month of Spanish lessons through Sarah's Spanish School (81). Designed for kids ages kindergarten through sixth grade, it is interactive, immersive, and requires no books. This comes highly recommended by other parents and is just a wonderful way to test out the subject and see if it's right for the family without having to throw down any cash.

Although this is directly aimed at children, there are more and more opportunities opening up for parents who wish to take on a new skill. First Frets (82) offers online homeschool guitar and ukulele lessons for any period of life. They have students as young as five all the way through retirement age. Best of all, they offer in-house discounts for home educators who sign up at conventions. My family was offered a 50 percent discount for the monthly plans, both single-student or for the entire family. That is a *lot* of savings. Especially considering that my husband has always wanted to really know the ukulele inside and out.

Many people don't know just how many great learning resources are available for homeschoolers. Conventions provide a stage for all of them so they can reach out to the families who will utilize them. This brings everyone together in a real-world setting without having to dig through websites or biased opinions.

As if that isn't enough, sports clubs that offer youth programs for homeschoolers specifically welcome anyone to come and check out their services. Tennis (83), basketball (84), and volleyball (85) are all eye-catching, especially for me, being that my youngest daughter used to play bitty ball, and is now a volleyball player who adores training and got her first competition experiences in 2021. Sports clubs exclusively made for homeschoolers are opening up nationwide. As home education grows more popular, so does the need for community activities designed to cater to the values of parents who are more involved in their children's learning processes.

For parents who wish to focus on more academic extracurricular activities, speech & debate clubs (86), and other study-focused groups like the Foundation for Individual Rights in Education, or F.I.R.E. (87)—which hosts an annual free-speech essay scholarship contest—cater to homeschooling families because most of these organizations know just how involved home educators are and need that kind of support to thrive. So, many families have different reasons for taking the homeschooling route that organizations like these are ready to give them a voice. The longer parents talk with the vendors and gain more information on expanded homeschooling programs, the more confidence they have in their ability to teach and properly provide the best education possible for their children.

Knowing that some parents choose to homeschool because their children have special needs, I was touched to know that Special Needs Tutors (88) often frequents these conventions to provide the additional support that some families need. They are the only organization that specializes in aiding special-needs students. After having met some home educators who live with the added struggles of having to meet special needs, it's just good to know this exists to help pass on the word, or remember, should any of my children need that form of assistance in the future.

Most everyone is welcoming, and the main focus is sharing homeschooling materials for students from pre-school through high-school age, but for all the vendors catering to grade school through high school, there are plenty of colleges that come through looking to recruit homeschooled students. Most of them are faith-based, but they are so welcoming (and reminded me personally) that regardless of any social stigmas that may be attached to children who are homeschooled, universities know better. They are friendly, informative, and a bit more conservative, so parents like me who wouldn't allow my kids to touch Yale (89) or Harvard (90) with a twenty-five-mile toothpick—based on their inability to help students to support simple American values like free speech and due process—these options are invaluable.

Places like Simpson University (91), Harding College (92), and even more explorative higher education options like Momentus (93) are all proud to receive homeschooled students. Momentus specifically offers an education that has spiritual ties but is also nature-based, so they work to take students out into the world for hiking, rock climbing, and other adventures that instill survival skills. That is something that many children could utilize in the future.

Any program that gets kids back outside and exploring life first-hand is something I wish to support. Technology is great, but with so many screens and sedentary educational practices expanding, it is a major focus for plenty of homeschoolers to ensure that our kids can identify trees, know which berries are poisonous or not, and what kind of mushrooms you can find in the forest and eat without getting sick. These skills have waned to such a degree in public settings that more nature-involved homeschool studies are on the rise. Parents who pay attention recognize that it's not healthy to be so disconnected from the trees just outside our homes, and the market knows that.

Animal studies are also of interest because they help connect science and learning with children who just like learning about different creatures. Cub Creek Science Camp (94) hosts children's camps that immerse students in nature and science and give them safe animal encounters so they can learn and experience connecting with the natural world through activities instead of just textbooks and classrooms. This camp is a bit pricy, but for homeschoolers who can save up, it's one of those resources that may just be worth it. Parents like me, who struggled with sitting still and taking tests all the time, can understand just what kind of resource a place like this is. I wish I'd been able to go there as a child, so working to give my kids the option to attend is something I'm set on.

Yet, not everyone is that gung-ho. For less costly nature experiences, the World Bird Sanctuary (95) is a fan of homeschoolers and was at our area's most recent convention promoting different programs to draw in families and children who are curious about animals and the natural connections we all host. Though I personally get giddy at just the idea of being able to hang out with some birds, I know that's not the case for all homeschoolers. For parents who want to encourage outdoor excursions without specified animal studies, Trail Life USA (96) is another exciting group providing outdoor learning experiences that are more focused on strength and achievement than single animal studies.

This is tailored specifically to boys since so many young men struggle in school. It's a great scouting group that provides an alternative to the increasingly "woke" Boy Scouts of America organization, and confronts the social and political issues that have arisen from boys who have been purposefully disconnected from their masculinity. They are Christian-based, which only means that they have a certain moral code that often benefits homeschoolers from all walks of life. That means so much to us, and Trail Life USA appeals to us mainly because they are focused on allowing boys to be strong, independent, masculine leaders without removing God from the equation.

As the mother of two young boys, I could fill a continent with my grievances against modern misandry. Everywhere I look, it seems that boys are being emasculated and vilified for their nature. Boys don't learn the same way girls do. Their brains are biologically different. From the verbal passageways connecting thought into words, to a desire for experiments and physical activity, boys require more tangible outlets to pour their energy into, and so many homeschoolers have chosen to educate their boys themselves because their sons suffer in the factorized institutionalized learning industry.

As more and more vendors and organizations tackle this situation and work to give young males the boyhood experiences and materials that will help them achieve success, finding helpful information on the subject is easier than ever. While wandering through the convention crowd my husband stumbled upon the book *Raising Resilient Sons* by Colleen Kessler EdM, at one of the booths and instantly bought it. It seems that plenty of parents are concerned about the attack on masculinity. Boyhood is under more scrutiny than ever, and for that reason, young males are suffering from confidence issues and a lack of direction or purpose. Homeschooling conventions are not government-regulated or corporate-affiliated like many public schools and after-school programs. As such, there is more freedom to display, distribute, and discuss these controversial topics in a truly open-minded educational environment.

Independent publishers and teachers alike are finding more solutions to the problem on their own than within government systems. The power of private education can be felt throughout every turn of homeschooling conventions. The vendors each offer their specialties, along with some freebies and maybe a little candy (my kids enjoy a few little sugar spikes), but there is so much more to these conventions than just the main selling room. All throughout the convention centers, speakers, workshops, and special events take place to offer guidance, instruction, and sometimes just a few laughs. A lot of the vendors offer workshops or get up and speak. This is their time to truly connect with their homeschooling audience and explain what they're all about.

It's a great opportunity for authors to share their stories and why their material is geared toward home educators directly. At the last convention that my family attended, we were able to talk about the fun children's picture book *The Beard Ballad* by Harold Cronk. The foreword was written by Phil Robertson—yes, the *Duck Dynasty* guy—and Robertson recorded a video message for everyone who wished to attend to see. It was pretty moving. Inspirational tales of the American Dream often are, but what really gave this event its extra oomph was the fact that everyone who attended was given a free copy of the hilarious hardcover book.

There are plenty of free books in the world. Parents can find them often if they just look, but some of them are not exactly high-quality. Honestly, I've found plenty of free books that you couldn't pay me to read, let alone give to my children as they continue absorbing information and processing it to make sense of the world around them. Thankfully, *The Beard Ballad* was nothing like that. Its hard-cover design is professional, the layout is exquisite, and the story is one that my boys love.

In the spirit of gifting homeschooled children the freedom to be themselves, this tale is a book about father/son bonding during No Shave November. I don't want to spoil the ending for anyone, but my husband's only complaint was that December involved a razor, but even so, the book is about so much more than beards. It's a hilarious story that displays the importance of male bonding and allowing young boys to embrace their masculinity.

Being given resources like this, for free, is not uncommon at conventions. They are the place to find all the deals and steals. Homeschoolers definitely benefit from attending one for a single afternoon.

Workshops and speaking events often have free gifts, but when they include books, I'm always front and center. Each workshop and speaking engagement is unique. Most of the workshops provide insight into featured teaching practices and principles. From ways to keep children engaged in math lessons throughout their educational career, time management, and understanding online courses, nearly every topic imaginable is covered. Community-based efforts like these are not secretive or exclusive; they're happily transparent and eager to share information because it benefits everyone to do so.

Most of the people running workshops are homeschoolers themselves, or plenty of them, were successfully homeschooled. That in and of itself helps to provide a positive atmosphere where parents can get acquainted with the various lifestyles and approaches that make homeschooling, even on a budget, a successful endeavor. Some are geared toward moms or dads specifically because we often have different concerns and strengths to offer our children together. No matter if one parent facilitates in home learning over the other, both parents hold so much influence that it's nice to have mom-to-mom discussions and allow fathers to come together in an environment where they are appreciated and encouraged to assert their leadership skills, instead of being told to step down and let the women do the work for them (which seems oddly backward, even though that is considered a "progressive" modern-day approach to many educational and career settings).

These interactive experiences, coupled with a bevy of workshops, connect faith and learning, others go on to tackle the awkwardness of puberty. Learning disabilities are also addressed in some formats, and I especially appreciate that because I'm dyslexic. Being so and having the ability to recognize that my youngest daughter's school work and abilities resemble my own gives me the option to guide her through her frustrations with understanding, whereas in the public education system, I suffered.

Listening to speakers get up in front of a crowd and familiarize everyone with the common issues that home educators and/or students face throughout the learning process and how to overcome these obstacles is refreshing. Parents walk out feeling as if they are not only prepared for what's to come but also destined to be in their position. A greater sense of purpose comes with these insights, and they are all part of the convention admission at no additional charge.

These workshops and speakers all host such specialized information that as many as eight of the events run at the same time, in various rooms, to offer everyone a chance to reach their audience. The allotted times go very fast. Even conventions that stretch on for days seem to whip by in a whir of lessons and a love of learning, teaching, and doing.

Best of all, sometimes big names are attached as the grand finale. Just this past season, in 2022, Dr. Carol Swain (97) closed out the Great Homeschool Convention in South Carolina and Texas. She was also set to speak in Ohio. Swain is a known television commentator who faithfully believes in the American dream. Her commitment to empowering others to better themselves was sparked from her own struggles where she raised herself up from being a teenage mother and high-school dropout to a successfully respected university professor.

As a black woman in the current political climate, she doesn't fall prey to identity politics and instead supports strong homeschooling families for their efforts to raise healthy, happy students who avoid classroom bias. She has written a number of best-selling books, which warn of the dangers of Critical Race Theory, the importance of faith in America, and cultural relativism. Parents who are able to meet women like Dr. Carol Swain and discuss her appreciation of homeschooling find themselves in a better mind frame for teaching.

Then, there was another big name attached to the 2022 tour. Tucker Carlson (98) closed out the Ohio convention, discussing Homeschooling & Today's Political Climate. This single-location event was highly anticipated. Plenty of people know the name, so some parents even travel to hit the different convention sites out of their home state. This Fox News host isn't afraid to voice his opinion while reporting on or calling out mass-scale hypocrisy in our government system, so one cannot deny his notoriety.

My husband wanted to travel to see him, but being on a budget, we had to examine our priorities. It's valuable to us to hear from different speakers, but we've been doing this home-education thing for so long now that we have a pretty good handle on it. We know what to anticipate and are easily able to adjust when new obstacles pop up.

I'm also conscious of the political divide. It's true that a lot of homeschool convention speakers are conservative. Homeschooling itself is, by nature, a more individualized concept and caters to more traditional ideals. That doesn't mean that liberals or centrists aren't welcome. I do my best to be a centered individual, not opposed to healthy debate and consideration for the arguments of people who respectfully disagree with me. Thankfully, in my experience, politics don't often come up at these events as a talking point, and even when they do it is lighthearted and presented as more of a banner in the background to be flown for the sake of freedom of religion, speech, and so on.

Parents who attend homeschooling conventions are adults, and we know how to get along with others. We want to get the best bang for our buck and don't often go seeking conflict. We don't have time for that. We're too busy sniffing out deals and saving our kids' money, so when it comes to convention special events, these are more unifying because homeschoolers generally tend to focus on what's best for their children, and that's having fun learning and finding your place within the community. Again, most special events come with the admission price without any additional fees. These can feature family-oriented musicians, clean comedians, or a "mom's night out" with snacks, games, and girl-talk.

Being able to bring the entire family to a concert isn't easy with a big family, but homeschooling conventions are up for the task. They cater to us, and in return, we keep coming back. It's part of that give-and-take that's come up before.

For families that prefer something a little tamer, sitting down to hear a comedian tell jokes about being homeschooled and homeschooling with a light-hearted whimsy offers everyone time to relax and forget the pressures they are under. These simple entertainment experiences remind us to smile and enjoy the process as we go—because it goes pretty fast. Then, and I may be biased here again, but because I'm a mom and I work and teach and rarely get time to sit or truly ponder everything, events designed for moms or dads to come together and just enjoy supporting each other are so very special. I guess that's why it's called a "special" event. Either way, having access to a few hours of snacking while playing games and discussing parenthood here and there is wonderful. I haven't done any dads-only events, being a mom, but I can say that exploring all things maternally involved with other homeschooling mothers completely rounds out a convention experience.

Homeschoolers look forward to these sorts of conventions because they offer the whole package. Parents can literally walk in and find everything they need to successfully homeschool their children. They can purchase their entire curriculum at a convention, or just pick up a few supplies. Having all of these options and the ability to see other families happily doing the same thing is such a joy. It is well worth the cost of admission and a perfect start to building the next year's lesson plans.

Since so many of us need plenty of time to lay out each year's courses, most homeschooling conventions are held in the springtime. It's a perfect season. The days are growing longer. It's getting warmer, and everyone is dying to get out of the house. My children enjoy coming with, and I enjoy having a few days with everyone, but going back alone or with your spouse and leaving the kids with a babysitter can offer the full effect.

However parents choose to approach a homeschooling convention, they will find countless bargains and free resources. That is something every parent can use. Not only this but they will find themselves more connected to the community. Taking the time to discuss homeschooling with others makes it more approachable. First-time families get a lot of their questions answered while returning veterans can seek out those hot buys that are so essential to retaining students' focus.

These social events get everyone out and connecting through their common links, and that is a bond that teaches so much to everyone. Home educators and their children leave better prepared, and beyond that, they find a stronger sense of duty to the cause of education and its place in the world. It's such a great feeling to walk into a building and find everything you need, even some materials you never dreamed existed.

It's so enriching, it makes parents like myself want to give back. When I hear others voicing concerns or looking for direction like I did when I first started homeschooling, I think about helping out. That's why I began writing this book—because so many people expressed a concern that they cannot afford homeschooling while others perpetuated this farce that "homeschooling is expensive." It truly doesn't have to be very costly. It all depends on what families plan to do and how they approach their studies.

Having come from a poor background and executing a strict homeschooling budget, I know that home education is a bargain that can be built on any means. Even if parents don't wish to frequent conventions, there are plenty of other ways to expand children's knowledge of their place in the world and allow them to extend their care and understanding in an effort to learn through more social means.

Sure, when homeschooled children are young, most of their instruction is done within the confines of our own four walls, but as they grow older, other pursuits can be added to benefit the educational process without costing anything. Community-based efforts, like charity work in particular, is of great interest and have been a tremendous teaching tool for my children.

Giving back to one's community—and the world in turn—is something young people often crave. They look for ways to use what they know to help others, and that youthful intelligence is something to be applauded and encouraged with guidance from parents. While homeschooling, we host the power to truly raise empathetic, charitable, pillars of the community. It's an honest, noble ideal that starts with a simple effort that doesn't have to cost a thing but a little time, and that is charity. So, let's leave the convention center and check out volunteer opportunities and fundraising ideas for students and parents to share.

CHARITY WORK

One of the best things about homeschooling—and doing so on a budget—is that families can teach about giving back to the community. Not everyone has the means to donate to causes for a single payment, let alone set up a regular recurring offer, but children always find creative ways to raise money, and they do love to volunteer their time.

Home educators have the ability to schedule these kinds of events or experiences whenever they wish instead of having to work around rigorous Monday-through-Friday public schooldays. Because I came from a low-income background, it's important to me that my family grows and thrives, but it's just as important that we give whatever we can. Time or money, clothes, canned goods, and/or gently-used household items, giving whatever we can give is a regular practice.

Since children quickly learn the value of helping others, these are perfect class projects. From lemonade stands and bake sales and tutoring or helping pack care packages, most charitable organizations always need help. The smaller and more localized the better. Like co-ops and homeschooling itself, home-grown charities are less likely to handle so much income that fraud becomes a concern. The leaders of local charities aren't usually pulling in hundreds of thousands of dollars in income like some of the national and global charities.

For example, the CEO of UNICEF USA, a leader in children's charities makes $620,000 per year (99). Now, this is less than one percent of the organization's total income, but for those of us making under $50,000 a year, the question of ethical salaries for charity leaders is a major concern. I understand that heading a global effort to help children may be taxing, but even if the CEO's salary were cut in half, the extra money could aid millions of more lives.

In 2020, the CEO of the Humane Society made $400,000 (100). Yet, the price of adopting a dog with their services has gone through the roof (101). When we adopted our dog from them, it was $300, and though he was supposed to be de-wormed, he was full of hook worms and needed multiple treatments that they refused to pay for. That didn't seem very humane to me.

So, picking and choosing the right charities matters. As families work with them, they learn who is truly fighting for a cause and who is sadly profiting off of the kindness of others. In truth, there are many wonderful organizations looking for aid. Asking children what they're interested in helps spark their excitement to get involved.

Though most charities don't allow young children to volunteer, kids are always encouraged to raise funds. My daughters begged to start an annual lemonade stand to donate to one of our favorite shelters, Open Door Animal Rescue (102). It's a no-kill shelter that always needs supplies and support. So, we set up and had a great time serving our neighbors. Cars pulled up, and people stopped and expressed their happiness at seeing children taking the initiative. A local police officer even came by to support the cause, and the children were so happy to talk about why they wanted to help.

That first stand raised over $100. It was highly encouraging and taught the kids so much about handling money and making sure to do the right thing with their funds, and it prepared them for more successes. As they get older, they now raise even more. At the start of summer every year, the kids go out and set up. I make the lemonade myself, squeezing lemons and mixing in sugar and water the old-fashioned way. Last year, the kids made close to $300, so they split it up between charities. It's a family event where everyone works together to raise funds, and that's something homeschoolers know a lot about.

Because we live on a tight budget, these kinds of student-led fundraisers not only teach fiscal responsibility but also math and communications skills. Even my shy eldest loves talking to her patrons. It has been such a great experience through the years that the children keep brainstorming ways to help other causes. The most recent idea is to host a "Black Cats' Lives Matter" bake sale and donate to the Black Cat Rescue (103), and just to keep the theme running, the kids were wanting to do an "All Dogs' Lives Matter," for Stray Rescue of St. Louis (104).

As the children get older and grow more aware of political divides and issues, they take on their individual views of them. I thought the idea of taking two opposing political ideologies and inserting them into sweet middle-ground issues might be fun, but the jury's still out on that. Whether or not we host these events depends on the children's dedication, our community, and so on, but either way, giving makes them feel good about themselves and teaches them the value of remembering others. It also eases the disappointment about not being able to volunteer at many shelters on their own yet.

I have been allowed to bring my girls along while caring for the cats at one rescue but only as observers. So many animal shelters are afraid of the liability of placing child volunteers near unpredictable animals that many do not permit anyone under the age of 12 to sign up, even with a parent's consent and supervision. Not being overly litigious myself, I brought my daughters and taught them to be calm and let the cats come to them. They were just there to tag along and sit with the cats while I cleaned cages and fed everyone, and if a friendly kitten just happened to sit in their lap or play with them, it was no issue.

Animal advocacy groups are a noble cause, but because they have a lot of age restrictions, humanitarian aid is also something that interests the kids. About twice a year we go through the toy boxes and pull out things the children don't play with anymore. We check everyone's clothes and reorganize the basement to find items that could get better use with someone who will appreciate and use them. This is a good way to free up space for new learning materials and so on.

We used to donate these things to Goodwill, but they seem to run more like a corporation than a charity nowadays. The CEO was criticized for making over $800,000 a year back in 2012 (105). Finding their current numbers has proven difficult, but the competing charity thrift store St. Vicent de Paul (106) is said to pay between $100,000 and 125,000 to its CEO (107).

Local thrift stores are our preference, but if choosing between these two, St. Vincent de Paul, is our choice. Every family should always do what works for them in their community, especially when their kids want to help out, but there are so many ways home educators can encourage their children to be charitable that the options are endless. My eldest loves babies and young children. She always asks about what it was like when I volunteered for the St. Louis Crisis Nursery (108) because she wishes to do so when she's old enough. She loves babies and getting involved with an organization that helps mothers in crisis, or even those who just don't have a support system and need childcare; it's something she is highly interested in, but because they often deal with small children who are likely to have suffered from poverty, neglect, or even abuse, volunteers must be eighteen years of age.

My eldest cannot wait for the day she can help out and rock the babies or play with children who are displaced. It reminds me of the senior high-school girls who specifically volunteered there because they were planning to get degrees in early-childhood education or just wanted some experience caring for babies and little kids. Those kinds of lessons are better built through experience and so knowing that option is there, it's something that can further aid homeschoolers with children who hold similar interests.

I do always work to be honest and realistic about volunteering, though. There is a bit of heartache that comes with caring for animals or children who may have been put in harm's way and who you will never see again once they've been helped. Yet, again, this is another life lesson that all students need to learn as they grow into adulthood, and learning how to focus on helping over worrying promotes better mental health and future successes.

This form of maturity takes time and is better guided by parents. As my children mature, part of our education experience involves discussing more serious issues and offering both sides of every issue to give the children their own ability to find common ground and think for themselves. It's another great benefit of homeschooling that requires no materials and no funding. Since my eldest has reached an age where politics interests her, she has taken an interest in the ever-pressing abortion argument. She believes that life is precious. Her knowledge of fetal development is extensive since I home-birthed her three younger siblings, and she's a pro-life advocate. Her belief that children are a blessing and not a burden led her to ask me about a Birthright (109) billboard we passed on the highway.

I had never fully researched the organization and didn't know exactly what they did, so we looked into them together. We learned they offer counseling and aid for women experiencing an unexpected pregnancy without receiving any government funding in order to uphold their missing to give women more options than just abortion. They provide free health care services to any mother in need and even help them to find good adoption services if the mother believes she cannot raise the child.

This is a cause that my daughter was eager to join. The charity is not used to middle-school-aged girls asking to volunteer and wanted to know why it was important to her. She simply put it, "Because I want to help women take care of their babies."

That is a fair stance that I wholly support. No matter where anyone stands on the abortion issue, women should always be offered more choices than just the common "abortion is healthcare" idea. If abortion is healthcare, then so is giving a baby up for adoption—or finding a way to love and nurture it. Being able to articulate that and stand up for her beliefs has been a learning experience in itself, but her philosophy has led both of us to volunteer and pack layette care bags for expectant mothers through the Birthright organization.

Just branching out and doing something new that is helping the community is something that enriches our understanding of the world and reinforces the idea that learning doesn't start and stop in a scheduled classroom session. Being able to express themselves and stand up for their beliefs is something that becomes very real when helping children do volunteer work.

Not to go on too much about this recent development in my daughter's life, but she feels it is her duty to help out because she so strongly cares about protecting babies at all stages of life. It was her idea, and I'm proud to see how she dedicates herself.

This is an experience that she will carry with her all throughout her life. It costs us nothing and provides so much purpose and love. Much like all the volunteer hours I've put in at various shelters and groups, this work is helping her become an adult. That's something I wish was a regular part of public schools: charitable endeavors. The annual canned food drives and car washes don't fully present the heart of the issues people face in adulthood. Children grow and change with more personal acts of care. They become who they were meant to be when given opportunities like volunteer work.

Of course, not all charitable acts are as dramatic or deeply woven. Some are lighthearted and fun but just as important. Older homeschooled students often make great tutors or teaching aids. It is a role that benefits both the student teaching and those who are learning from them. By teaching other children what they already know, they solidify their understanding of different subjects while also finding new ways to communicate their understanding to help others learn.

Math especially is a course that many students struggle with. Because it is more analytical and focuses on pattern recognition instead of more physically connected subjects like science and writing, there is always a need for math tutors. Homeschooled students who excel in this subject can work with other children regardless of whether they go to public school, private school, or are also homeschooled.

This is a route that rewards students for tackling an unpopular subject with enthusiasm, but even for students who don't wish to tutor, just being given the opportunity to teach a small group of younger children is a charitable act that broadens their horizons and helps them empathize with their parents and other educators.

My eldest is a math whiz but she hates it. She wants nothing to do with entering a math field when she grows up nor does she appreciate the suggestion to tutor math. Despite this, she *does* love helping her sister with vocabulary skills and reading to her younger brothers and cousins.

Her little sister is also a fan of coaching younger kids. When smaller children ask for her help or wish to learn about the things she likes her eyes light up and she teaches them using a unique brand of storytelling that is both engaging and insightful. All children have the ability to pass on information to better their peers or younger students. Sometimes, it takes a simple trip to the park, others, they can seek positions volunteering at summer camps or through other community activities.

At the stable where my eldest goes to summer camp, they're always looking for older girls to help young riders get used to caring for horses and become comfortable being safe while having fun with them. Those who do are offered discounts on their own lessons, so it's a wonderful give-and-take that lowers costs without having to cut anything out. Plenty of places are willing to work out these kinds of deals, even if they're not offered on a regular basis, and children are eager for fulfilling roles like these. Once they get started it's hard for them to stop because they build such great relationships and see how their actions influence the success of other children.

It truly is a gift and a blessing to be able to impart this as part of our family's teaching philosophy. Because so many homeschoolers spend extra time on lessons that teach ethics and community service, adding in faith-based elements may seem only natural. Now it must be said that in my state, religious teachings cannot be counted for our main schooling hours, which there is a minimum requirement for, but because we have a year-round teaching schedule in our home, that leaves plenty of time to reach out to others on a spiritual level. So, parents should be aware of their local government and at least get somewhat familiar with the terms set for homeschooling families, but once all of that is known, there are plenty of ways to meet requirements and still create lessons that cater to your family's specific life and faith system.

Religious homeschoolers are proud of the spiritual work their children do. Whether working within their church, synagogue, mosque, meditation circle, or even at a faith-based retreat, picnics, food drives, and other events help others to connect and build a stronger community. Helping the needy and offering support for our fellow humans is just something that goes hand-in-hand with homeschooling because parent educators see first-hand how eager their children are to do some good in the world. This coincides with a lot of religious and spiritual organizations, as that is usually their main goal as well.

Being able to blend that into the educational experience without having to spend thousands of dollars on a religious private school is something many of us treasure. Some private schools offer discounts to families based on income, but even so, tuition rates are often comparable to college fees, so finding that balance between raising our children with strong faith and values without going into debt is much easier through the practice of homeschooling. When I was in high school, I remember a prayer circle club formed with some of the students, and the question of whether or not that should be allowed on public school ground was raised.

I found it odd at the time because I've always strongly believed in the principles of freedom of religion that allows families in the United States to worship as they choose without fear of persecution. It seemed odd to me that some non-religious parents mistook freedom *of* religion as freedom *from* religion, which are two very different concepts.

There is nothing more beautiful than discussing homeschooling options with people of faith. I've yet to meet a family that demeans me and mine for our spirituality, and in return, I would never do so to others. Being able to pray before, during, or after school is a child's right.

Going further back into one of my earlier schooling experiences, I used to pray before I ate lunch. It was a regular practice, one I still uphold to a degree, but one day, a school administrator came up to me and told me that I was not allowed to pray in the cafeteria. This was in a suburb of St. Louis,

Missouri, the Bible Belt.

My mother was so upset when she heard what happened that she contacted the school and complained. She explained that it was none of their business whether a student chooses to pray or not. Although they apologized and no one stopped me after that, the memory remains. If my mother had not said anything, I would have most likely been prohibited from praying before I ate in school and others may have been as well. I think of that often when religious freedoms are being debated—and also when my children meditate on beautiful days when we go outside to play after lunch.

These experiences have been in the background of my social character for years. They helped me to question the current system. I have found that despite all the factorized learning I was subjected to, education is much more than sitting at a desk and staring at a teacher. It is learning from others through actions and understanding. There is nothing that drives self-awareness and the awareness of others like volunteer work and other home-based educational practices that don't draw lines between faith and community. This is a fact that has guided me through many years of homeschooling with very little money (but all the benefits of intelligent thoughtful children).

As the years go by, I am more conscious of how children mature into young adults and the fact that as we reach the end of our homeschooling journey, there is no other option I wish to pursue in helping them finish their primary and secondary schooling. Home education has served us well. Beyond the focus of charity and volunteer work lies the added option of workforce training—which is another skill-building form of education that home-educator parents can help their children explore once they reach the mid-late teen years, and *that* adds a whole other element to the budget because apprenticeships, shadowing, and internships lead to those first jobs, which can add to the budget instead of deducting from it.

Workforce training lends our young adults the ideals of building their own dreams and housing them with the knowledge they retain. It gifts them experience and a taste of what's ahead. Mainly, it prepares them in ways that other schooling programs never will.

WORKFORCE TRAINING

s public school enrollment declines and staffing shortages (110) occur across the nation, many people are looking for solutions. Some states are now dropping college requirements for state jobs (111) while others incentivize student work programs (112), and homeschoolers know the importance of hands-on learning, so why wouldn't we seek out opportunities for our children to gain some workforce training before they graduate? It's a perfect opportunity to mix learning with experience, which offers new lessons that our children will carry with them through the rest of their lives.

Workforce training can seem like a heavy subject, but in truth, it can be as simple or involved as home educators wish. From take-your-child-to-work opportunities to shadowing, first jobs, and more, gifting students with some real-work experiences helps them understand what their education is all about. No, the sole purpose of learning about the world isn't just to gain a career path, but it's a common endeavor that serves students well and encourages them to study no matter what kind of successes they wish to meet.

When I was a kid, I loved going to my parents' workplaces. My dad was a construction worker, so it was cool to see all the equipment and how things got built so fast. I marveled at unfinished homes. Looking at all the beams and pieces that had to be placed just right to create a solid structure enhanced my love of geometry.

My mother tried her hand at many things throughout my childhood. Sitting with her when she worked for a bank or helping her finish stocking shelves when she worked for a hardware store filled me with an appreciation of what she did. It was this variety that gave me a better understanding of multiple options and also allowed me to take comfort in the fact that even adults change careers after they've decided what they wish to do with their lives.

Having learned so much from these rare occasions meant so much to me that I wish to offer similar situations to my own children. Passing these kinds of experiences on to my sons and daughters is something that excites me as much as it intrigues them. Just as my interest in growing up and working hard increased during these visits, my children are always eager to come to my desk and watch the magic happen. Whether I'm preparing a freelance article or at the office where I write for a local business, their presence is such a joy.

My husband's position is quite different. He delivery drives on the weekends. His job is all about ensuring everyone gets what they ordered—and quickly. The kids are always begging him to take them with. They love car rides but also seeing how adults act when they're "on the clock."

What may seem like mundane busywork to parents is fun and interesting to our children. It's good for them to explore what we do and have the ability to observe our processes. Many homeschoolers have a one-income household, so sharing how the "bread-winner" makes a living is also a good time to educate children about budgets and how to balance effort, time, money, and so on.

For homeschooling parents who are unable to bring a child to work, setting up a pretend business in the house and teaching them to operate it is a creative approach that displays how our education is so much more than just bookwork. A project like this doesn't need to be too fancy or elaborate. Utilizing household supplies can keep the budget on track while opening up new activities. Anyone with an oven can help their children pretend to run their own bakery. Or even just mixing up some uncooked candy for pretend sales can enrich an afternoon lesson on commerce.

Once children grow old enough to branch out, parents can contact local businesses or a family friend and see about shadowing opportunities. These are just simple planned shifts where older students can go to work with someone who holds a position in a profession they appreciate. They then get to follow the worker around and observe all the tasks that make up the job. It's pretty self-explanatory. Our students get to become someone's "shadow" in order to learn and witness productivity for themselves. It's a great way to get older kids out and ready for their first job without making them apply too quickly.

Shadowing is easier to do within small businesses. Instead of having to worry about corporate chains for approval and all sorts of national business red tape, the owners are more easily contacted and agreeable. Many of us know someone who runs a local restaurant or shop. These community ties help home educators if they just ask.

If a student enjoys shadowing, they may wish to take on an apprenticeship or internship. It all depends on the profession, but when I worked as a veterinary assistant at the Clarkson Wilson Veterinary center in Chesterfield, Missouri, my boss was happy to allow high-school and even some mature middle-school students to volunteer and help organize the office or care for the office pets. It was encouraging to see students come in ready to help. They wanted to work, and this is not uncommon; many children still seek out in-field experiences to better themselves.

Apprenticeships may be a bit outdated in most fields, but even some carpenters can still use an assistant, and my family even knows a couple of old wood workers at our farmer's market who love to pass on their wisdom. So, home educators shouldn't be afraid to discuss these prospects within their community and seek outside career training for their students. These positions may not pay, but they do afford a lot of educational growth.

Internships, similarly, provide students with the ability to get some real-world hands-on experience. They are trained and expected to show up on time, fulfill their obligations, and work well with others. These were much harder to find before I became a parent, but now thanks to the Internet, there are even plenty of remote internships popping up in tech fields, publishing, and news media. Some require minimum ages, so older students who are nearing the end of their homeschooling journey are best suited for these opportunities, but they are there for parents to seek out. Plus remote internships have the added safety net of allowing students to fulfill their duties from home where their parents can monitor them as needed.

In addition, parents who make contacts and reach out first are more likely to find better positions in out-of-the-house scenarios. Taking that extra step to shoot off an email or make a call gets employers thinking. Where programs are lacking, one may be formed after interest is presented, so it's important for home educators to take the initiative.

Once a position is secured, how students handle these new challenges will vary. Homeschooling parents should be ready to offer support and trusted advice. Not every situation will meet success, but that in itself is a lesson they will carry with them as they navigate into adulthood. One of my main goals has always been to accept that my children might love something for a while but then move on to something greater. On the other hand, sometimes kids quit something they love and regret it later.

Moral support is one of the most important free benefits of homeschooling. All parents can offer this but none so greatly as home educators. Finding the balance between consoling children when they're just having a rough period and learning when they are truly unhappy and need to move on is another lesson that parents receive from their own practices.

Over time, this gets easier and it may be to a student's benefit to take on their first job. Experience is a great teacher. It helped me through a lot of turmoil and ensured my own safety and security when I faced homelessness during my senior year of high school. Because of my work history and experience, I was able to take care of myself (with moral support from some really awesome people).

Now that I'm a mother, I wish to use those painful experiences to help my children help themselves. I know that I may not always be able to be there for them. If something happens to me or my husband, I want to know they will thrive. That's something I think a lot of parents can relate to.

Of course, as a teacher, the prospect of allowing students to work may seem challenging. Having a job requires time and commitment. It's good to lay out some ground rules to make sure that the opportunity to work or take on internships and shadowing is clearly defined and that everyone involved is aware of their expectations. Some good boundaries to set are:

1. Students must keep up with their school work.
2. Students must appreciate the opportunity.
3. Students must apply themselves.
4. Students must know to ask for help if working becomes too overwhelming.

I don't generally have lists of rules for my children, but homeschooling has so many different possibilities, so a proper education has to come first and foremost. For students who wish to work before they're legal adults and before they're even old enough to get a driver's license, the laws will vary in each state. When I was young, student-workers had to be fifteen years of age or older and needed to acquire a worker's certificate (113). The rules and regulations that come with this certificate have slightly changed over the years but have the same purpose: to keep student workers and their employers safe and properly represented.

Worker's certificates are traditionally obtained through the public education system. The protocols are different in each state. For homeschoolers in Missouri, the process is similar. Children being taught at home who wish to work can do so at age fourteen or older, but they're subject to many restrictions. Instead of filling out a form through the public school system, homeschooling parents can obtain the work certificate application online or through the Department of Labor and will fill in the "Issuing Officer" section as the official who is allowing the work to be performed, and also have the student fill in their information. It seems very binding but isn't too intrusive.

Any student in my state who wishes to work under the age of fourteen must have their parent fill out a worker's permit. These are almost always for work in the entertainment industry. Since this isn't the norm, it's less of a focus but just as important to note.

Then comes the long list of rules & restrictions that youth workers and their employers must adhere to (114).

- Workers under sixteen cannot clean or power meat processors, operate bread slicers, or heavy machinery.
- They cannot load or unload trash and box compactors.
- They cannot drive to work.
- They cannot cook outside of the use of deep fat fryers, bake, handle hot oil or grease, work for any establishment which sells alcohol, or work in a freezer or meat cooler.
- They cannot work from ladders.
- No working during school hours.
- No working before 7 a.m.
- No working past 7 p.m. during the schoolyear.
- No working past 9 p.m. during summer break.
- No working more than three hours on school days.
- No working more than eight-hour shifts.
- No working more than six days a week.

These are pretty relatable. These rules are mainly to avoid liabilities and tragedy and to prevent employers from overwhelming children in the workforce. Safety and responsibility are the main goals for everyone involved. Employers need good workers. Home educators wish to know that their children will benefit from their working experiences, and students need to explore self-sufficiency without having to continuously compromise themselves or their security.

Limiting hours is a big concern for many parents. A simple weekend job at an ice-cream shop isn't difficult for a fourteen-year-old to enjoy and may teach them a few things parents can't. Those first jobs build mature social skills. As tweens grow into teenagers, they learn how to deal with conflict, exercise self-control, and work with others even when they don't mesh with each other.

Those social skills are not exclusive to work, but they are more necessary in a working environment. It was at the first job through which I learned how to handle disappointment or frustration without having an outburst. I had to find better ways to express myself in a professional environment when a co-worker and I disagreed. These are lessons homeschooling students learn at home and other social settings, but their impact becomes more evident to our children when applied in a job setting to ensure success during shifts.

Boundaries also become more defined. Students realize why appropriate language and discussion in a professional setting are crucial to healthy work relationships. At home, siblings argue and have to deal with each other, but they also know their brother and/or sisters enough to be more personal. While doing tasks at a job, deciding what personal information to share, and what to retain is a subject that cannot easily be taught at home. The philosophy can be studied, but putting discretion and manners into practice in the workplace with new people is a whole new scrapbook of experiences that needs filling.

When I look back on my first job, I think of it fondly. Even though it was tiring and sometimes very stressful, what I learned making salads at a local pizza shop instilled a love of working and earning my own way. Parents who are still wary of students working don't have to press the issue, but it would benefit everyone involved if they considered the child's homeschooling experience thus far.

If homeschooled students have already hosted events to raise money for charity and fulfilled hours of volunteer work, they are more likely to be prepared to take on that first job early on. It's worth looking into at the very least. Thankfully, most places that hire underage workers through state certificate and permit programs are generally service-based, so if a student gets hired and then struggles, they can resign without feeling like a failure because most service positions have higher turnover rates, and those experiences are also important for entering adulthood.

Students should be prepared to try out different positions without feeling as if they're obligated to continue working in a situation that just isn't right for them. In turn, they must also learn a balance—that no one loves their job every day. No matter how exciting a position is, some days are harder than others, and that life lesson is one in which parents can ease homeschooled students into with support for a summer job or even a short-term work program.

Short-term work is a great way to start. Those old-fashioned community-based jobs that were once a staple in society can still enrich the lives of children, especially those who are more connected to their community through homeschooling. Posting fliers for mowing lawns or offering baby-sitting services for neighbors, friends, and family eases everyone into work without long-term consequences. Then, from there, coaching a sports team for one session at the Y, or taking on a lifeguard position at a pool during the summer offers enough time to really dive into employment opportunities without drowning in all the expectations. Best of all these don't have costly work expenses like older-professional careers do.

Summer jobs grant students the ability to gain experience without balancing schoolwork, and best of all, many of these options hold the possibility of longer, steady work when students and their families are ready. Steady work can be tricky. Finding the right situation that works around shifting student schedules isn't always easy, but most service establishments are prepared to handle change.

It's my belief that all students should work in fast-food jobs first. This is just my humble opinion, but fast-food jobs are some of the most challenging yet low-paying positions out there. I always remind my kids that fast-food workers don't get paid low wages because they aren't working hard or providing a service to others, but because workers get paid based on how expendable they are. If anyone can do your job, you're less likely to be paid much more than others. By contrast, if you are highly skilled and competitive and not many people can do what you do, you make more because employers cannot replace you. This is learned first-hand while working at a fast-food restaurant. It doesn't take long for young workers to witness the turnover rate.

Fulfilling their duties at a hard fast-paced job where customers aren't always as kind as they could be also instills resilience. Whereas some of our children's co-workers may quit because they're having a bad day or because someone was mean to them, teaching children to at least finish their shift and put in their two weeks' notice before they resign is a respectable practice. They learn to appreciate the people who appreciate this form of work, which is another enriching part of working in fast food.

My first three or four jobs were in fast food, and because of my experiences there, I make sure to always be nice to the people making my food. Those are the sort of values that homeschoolers typically hold. Not only does working a first job in food service offer students a better grasp of society as a whole, but it also offers a stronger sense of economy. Working in fast food quickly teaches students to value their time and money, thus helping them to learn to be better budgeters and careful with how they spend what they make. There is also the added benefit that they are likely to appreciate all the budgeting work that parents put in for them as well.

Customer service jobs are other popular forms of employment for students. As they build their credentials and gain a stronger sense of self, homeschooled students may prefer to work in a store they enjoy buying from. This is a smart move because employee discounts alone help them to better afford a few extras instead of just relying on us as parents to always buy everything. Learning that balance and how to stretch their own dollar is invaluable.

I loved working at a clothing store when I was young because the discount helped me save money. I could dress well without going broke. This isn't something students easily learn from sitting in a classroom or even by following a homeschool curriculum. Eventually, our children have to get out and gain more, no matter how they're educated.

My first jobs were some of the most frustrating yet happy experiences of my life. I made friends of different ages and figured out how to balance work and education while still having fun and enjoying being young. So long as these opportunities are balanced with proper guidance and care, homeschooled teens will learn a lot, and best of all, they'll make a little bit of money to help further their interests, which just might ease your budgeting burdens. Even if it comes down to them buying their own sketchpads every so often, every little bit helps.

Working through learning is an educational experience that many students have to turn to as they enter adulthood and face college or trade schools. Even young adults whose parents squirreled away a college fund will quickly find just how expensive higher education can be. Thankfully, they won't have to worry about that too soon. It comes in due time.

Gaining an idea of what students wish to pursue once they finish school is something all parents should work toward, but homeschoolers have the added concerns of making sure they meet graduation criteria and determining what kinds of tests their students have to take to complete their education program in order to move on to bigger and bolder things.

So, before I close this out with my chapter on life after homeschooling—which includes college, trade schools, or taking time off to work, while we parents can finally take a well-earned, much-needed extended vacation—we're going to have to address all those things that creep up toward the end of high school: T-E-S-T-S. Yes, no matter how avant-garde our teaching styles are or aren't, our students have to make the grade to pass.

Colleges across the nation are dropping SAT and ACT requirements for admissions (115), so homeschoolers and their children should discuss what works best for their families. I'm too curious to see where my children score to avoid these traditional standards. Even so, these tests are costly, so if the budget gets too tight, they may not be something that everyone who is homeschooling on a budget will care to pay for anymore.

Just like the SATs and ACTs, GET or HiSET tests cost money. These are the exams that afford students their high-school equivalency paper. Some homeschoolers enroll their students in online schools so they can get a traditional diploma, which is also a nice option. Whether students get a job and wish to help pay for them or not, these tests are a large portion of passing their homeschool education, so the next chapter is all about exploring each of these different paths.

SATS/ACTS GED/HISET

Homeschooling can only go on for so long. Sure, plenty of parents would love to pretend to be college professors—and some of us are actually successful professionals who never run out of lessons—but eventually, students must graduate. They work hard to finish high school, and they deserve their proper due, but how to get them to that step has a few different approaches.

The traditional route is to, first, prepare teens for their SAT and ACTs and then have them finish their high school exams. After those are taken, some homeschoolers are advised to take their GED or HiSET tests. These exams must be passed in order to properly advance onward from high school and have that advancement universally recognized by employers and other institutions of learning. There are a few other routes that some home educators prefer. Even homeschooling parents who don't enroll their children in online homeschooling programs for every grade sometimes enroll their high school-aged children in online schools so they can receive a traditional diploma.

Although plenty of brick-and-mortar schools have published papers stating that GEDs and High School Equivalency tests don't hold as much weight as a high-school diploma, there have been no studies to confirm this. Nearly every college accepts GEDs or HiSETs, most businesses just want to make sure that their applicants have completed their high-school level courses, and even the stigma attached to these alternative routes has been diminishing as homeschoolers outperform their peers and graduate early. So, all the rhetoric pushing the fear that a GED or HiSET achievement isn't as good as a diploma may well just be propaganda published by schools that don't want to lose prospective students. They may also be basing their opinion on outdated information from decades past—or hearsay. Whatever the case, plenty of successful people are GED-holders (116).

In truth, a fifteen-year-old homeschooled student who has their GED and hours of community service work will easily outshine an eighteen-year-old high school graduate who is just applying because they're expected to. Circumstances always matter, and because high schools don't wish to see their students drop out and graduate early, they will continue to perpetuate the false idea that a high school diploma matters more than a GED, but the only thing that really matters to colleges, employers, and others, is that the person they are researching has an obvious work-ethic and commitment to the subjects they're pursuing.

In interviewing a few friends and family members who received their GED instead of a high-school diploma, I found that not a single one of them has been denied college admissions or a job based on that alone. This is great news for homeschooling parents and anyone with a gifted child who wishes to leave the public education system and graduate a year or two early. But all of these tests do cost money. Though a high school diploma is *not* free (no matter how many people will say it is), it's already paid for by our tax dollars, so budgeting for these tests is yet another expense that homeschooling parents must prepare for.

The SAT and ACTs have been a standard for college entrance for decades. Though they do differ, both display how students fare in math, reading, and writing. Only the ACTs measure science and essay skills in addition (117). The debate over whether tests actually serve to measure how much a student has learned, or whether they just display how good students are at taking tests has gone on for years, and because of this, a significant number of colleges recently stopped requiring SAT and ACT scores for their admissions process (118), but MIT—which was one of the first colleges to drop these tests—actually decided to reinstate them in spring of 2022 (119), so there are many factors to consider when determining whether or not to have students take these tests.

As a homeschooling parent myself, I believe it's important to prove that my children have received the best education possible, so I'm personally for taking these tests. My children are well aware of this. Because test-taking is a skill that is widely utilized for higher-education purposes, my husband and I have given our children some tests to ensure that they can handle the pressure that comes with filling in blanks and answering essay questions, but not every homeschooler believes this is the correct route for their children, and each parent has to do what is right for their family.

For those who choose to prepare their children for the SATs and ACTs, practice is key. Thankfully, there are free SAT prep tests available online (120). These practice tests offer students the opportunity to see what's in the test and how it works. It gives them a clear idea of the timing and information involved so they can better study and acquaint themselves with the process.

The ACTs are a bit more rigid. Their organization sells approved study guides that are pretty affordable when compared to the price of textbooks (121). A full set can still be obtained for around and even under $100. That may take a dent out of the budget, but it's well worth it for students who will be taking the ACTs because the tests themselves cost money, and although students can take both the SATs and ACTs multiple times, each test comes with its own fees.

Making sure to prepare students and offer them good test-taking tips and techniques like deep breathing and the process of elimination can ease test anxiety and help homeschooled students obtain the scores they desire. The tests themselves have varying fees. I was shocked to learn that the SATs haven't gone up in price from the time frame when I was in high school. They're set at $55 per test (122). Now, rushed results or phone results cost extra, but the test alone is still pretty affordable. The ACTs are as well, though they come with different options.

The ACT with no writing is, at the time of writing this book, $63 (123).

With the writing section, it's $88. Options to change the test information, register to take the exams late, change the date of the test, and more all come with additional fees, so parents need to be organized and prepare their students for studying and taking their exam when it is scheduled and how it's scheduled to avoid additional fees.

Both the SAT and ACT sites are closed, and testing is timed. They each take about three hours and must be completed within the allotted time frame. This can be stressful for our children, so making sure to focus on their needs above worrying over the cost of re-tests is advised.

Then, once it's over, it's over. At least for a time. The results are tabulated on their own scales. The SATs have a wider range of 40–1600 points, while the ACTs are a score of 1–36. Should students or parents find the scores too low, or students wish to retake the test, it isn't a bad option. Plenty of people do it just to try and outdo their previous score. It can be a way to beat their personal best and prove to themselves that they can do better, but honestly, students have a lot of studying to do, so that should always be determined on a case-by-case basis.

For example, my eldest loves reading and she's really good at sitting still and acing math tests. Her sister, on the other hand, prefers hands-on learning and experiments so what works for one will definitely not work for the other. Thankfully, home educators have the luxury to truly treat each child according to their specific needs and cater to that.

Whether homeschoolers push some or all of their children to take their SATs or ACTs isn't really the main objective in the grand scheme. Those tests may help in the future, or they may prove to be a waste of time for students who go directly into a trade. What really counts at the end of each child's homeschooling career is passing high school.

Sure, in theory, I could decorate a scepter and knight each of my children as valedictorian of the "Mom and Dad Academy," but it won't hold much weight outside of our house. What every home educator has to prepare for is honestly graduating their children through means that are universally accepted. There are multiple options here, and one does include a homeschool diploma certified by home educators, but it's not just a piece of paper; parents who take this seriously go to great lengths to ensure that their children obtain the proper knowledge to compete with their peers.

Traditional diplomas are not out of the question for homeschoolers. Parents can enroll their children in the online school of their choice at any stage in the educational process. So long as students do the work, pass high school courses, and meet all graduation requirements, they're able to earn a diploma and celebrate the end of their home education career.

But how do parents find these schools? And can they be trusted? Though I haven't enrolled any of my children in any online homeschool academies, and my husband and I don't intend for any of our children to enroll, the possibility is there. Like always, because every lesson starts at home, I've done my own research and also found it comforting to rely on the experiences of other homeschooling parents to fill in certain blanks.

Let's Homeschool Highschool's website offers a list of online schools that traditionally graduate students from high school with a diploma (124). In addition, there are also listings of free virtual high schools in nearly every state in the USA. (125). Picking and choosing the best online homeschooling option depends on what parents and students are looking for.

Home educators should take their time to research these various options and weigh the pricing with the benefits. Free virtual schooling sounds nice to some, but I'm usually skeptical of "free" classes because of certain political organizations (like zero population movements) that were introduced to me through "free" public school events and pushed their own biased agendas. Even so, there are some great options out there for parents wishing to go this route.

For families that don't wish to enroll students in online schools but still prefer a traditional diploma, they do have a personalized option. It has been noted by various sources that homeschoolers can simply administer their very own diploma based on whatever criteria they choose for their children. This means that graduation is solely at the parents' discretion. Then, for a small fee, home educators can design and personalize their own high-school diplomas under the name they give their homeschool (126). Parents who fully stand by their teaching, and the freedoms of at-home-learning may feel this is a good way to represent just exactly how serious and professional homeschooling is. Students who obtain diplomas from their parents aren't reported to find difficulty obtaining employment or even enrolling in college, so long as they have the credentials to back up their parent-made home-education diploma.

The idea of going this route definitely appeals to me as an educator. Instead of having to measure our children's understanding of their lessons through standardized tests, my husband and I can allow our kids to display their knowledge through projects, presentations, and other hands-on methods of displaying their knowledge. That being said, I find that if we were to go this route, SAT and ACTs seem a bit more important, though—just to prove to colleges and employers that our children can achieve high scores through conventional means. This comes down to my main goal as a mother, to ensure that my children are not stigmatized for being taught at home. Other parents may find that testing just isn't necessary for their children's future goals and a homeschool diploma is all they need.

This route may appeal to some home educators, but it doesn't suit everyone, and so, for parents who do not wish to enroll their children in online homeschooling programs to graduate them with a diploma or create their own home-education high-school degree, the good old-fashioned state-required exams are the next option. Depending on your area, the tests may or may not have been modernized. For many years, the GED (Generalized Education Development) tests have been taken to offer a degree similar to that of a high school diploma. In my state of Missouri, these have been replaced by the HiSET tests, which stand for High School Equivalency Tests.

These exams are easy to understand and simple to set up. Plenty of young athletes who graduate early obtain them at a young age so they can focus on their sport, and students who wish to graduate early (like my eldest) tend to rely on these as well. So, as long as unnecessary subjects like Female Yoga Fishing, or The History Of Hair Color In Mathematics do not enter into these tests—as much fun as they may or may not be for extra-curricular weirdness—they're the route that my family is intent on pursuing. Now, should politically biased identity subjects dominate, or even enter these state-run tests, we will have to reassess. One of the main reasons my family homeschools is to teach the core classes that will aid our children in finding success in adulthood. Math, science, reading, writing, history, and some customized interests are designed for each child. If the HiSET deviates from these standards, then we will change our plans, but for now, this seems to be the most universal, viable option for parents like me who prefer to finalize our children's homeschooling experience with an outside stamp of approval.

The GED test pricing differs per state (127). It can be taken online at home or in person. The in-person testing is done through an approved center and is actually less expensive, but the test's price is based "per subject." It is free in some states and ranges between about $20–$40 per subject, in most areas. It all just depends on the state administering the exam.

Just as each place has its own pricing, they also have their own set of rules for testing. Age requirements and conditions vary. In the state of Washington, students must be nineteen years old before they can test for their GED, but in Colorado, the age is seventeen years old. Most of these stipulations can be voided if a student has dropped out of high school or has a parent sign off on taking the exam underage.

In some states, students must prove that they are US citizens, while some require that the test be taken within the students' home state. In addition, some areas require students to take a practice exam before testing. This seems to be more common for online testing at home instead of exams that are taken at the approved testing centers, but again it all comes down to state regulations.

The HiSET tests in my home state of Missouri are similar to GED exams, but they're handled a little differently (128). Students must be sixteen and considered out of high school to take the test. Parents can press for earlier testing, but all students taking the exam must be a resident of the state. Practice tests are not required, but proof of identification must be shown before taking the evaluation.

The test itself is made up of five different subtests, which all cost $17.75

at approved testing sites, along with a $10 registration fee that is only required once every twelve months (129). This period includes students who many take their time retesting. The entire exam is $98.75 when taken at a testing center. The cost goes up if students chose to test at home for health or transportation reasons. Each subtest for the home exam is priced at $28.50 plus the state registration fee, totaling $151.25 for the entire set of exams done remotely.

The HiSETs were designed to be taken at a set location. Homeschoolers living on a budget may find that the discount for taking students to an approved test site is worth the trip. Like the SAT and ACTs the exams are given within a set time frame and results can be mailed, accessed online, or even obtained over the phone. Scores can be sent to colleges or employers, so they're easily accessible. Also, should a student fail, they can re-test. This is true for the GEDs as well because the main goal is for students to earn these degrees.

Students who properly prepare are expected to pass on their first exams, whether they are taking a GED test or the HiSETs. If a student fails their first GED test, they must retake, but they must do so in a test center, instead of virtually, and they are allowed at least one retake per subject each year (130). If a student doesn't pass the HiSETs on their first attempt, they are allowed to retake each subject twice within a single calendar year.

It's a lot to take in when just considering all the logistics, but in truth, the process is simple and easy to get through. Every retest is subject to the fees charged for the first attempt, so parents who choose this route for their homeschooled children should make sure to properly prepare them if they wish to save money and stick to a solid budget. Now, as a mother, I do wish to express that failure is often something children struggle with. Parents just getting into home education shouldn't look down on the prospect of failing at any stage, especially at the end of a child's high school career. When students are unable to make the grade, it just means that they need more time and further studies.

These tests all come with a lot of time and pressure. Most of them cost fees that add a financial pretense as well. Money is a concern for so many parents but especially homeschoolers, yet wisely budgeting and utilizing our funds to educate our children and propel them toward success is worth all the retesting fees we could ever pay.

There is a balance for each family that must be sought and attained on their own household terms. Just researching these tests and all of the options for getting a child through their home education journey is exhausting. Doing the work is . . . well, work! Yet, like all difficult tasks, it's incredibly rewarding.

Parents whose homeschooled children test high on the SATs or ACTs are thrilled with the results because they reflect on their ability to teach as much if not more so as they measure their children's success. However families decide to get their children through the end of their high school courses and commence their graduation, getting to that final point is something that cannot be described. The love and sense of accomplishment I've witnessed at homeschool graduation ceremonies is shared by parents and their children across all boundaries.

It doesn't matter if children earn a diploma from online homeschooling courses, their parents' own approved degree system, or the state-run GED/HiSET programs. What truly matters as our children finalize their primary and secondary education experiences is how they take all that they've learned and apply it to their future endeavors. Any parent who reads through this book and thinks, "This is too much," I want you to know that it is a LOT. But in truth, it isn't all piled on us at once. This is a long-term process that slowly leads toward a full well-rounded education based on the specific interests and values of parents and their children.

It doesn't take a genius to educate a child. It doesn't even take the most intelligent parent on the block. All you need is a plan and the will to put it into action. Part of that plan is building an honest budget, and being there for your kids. The rest is really filled in as you go. Experience is the best teacher, this is true for both homeschoolers and their students. Time and effort will breed confidence and ease students into graduation readiness. That's it.

Once graduation nears, students face young adulthood. College, trade schools, and jobs await. How these options are handled is up to them, but home educators hold more influence over what their children choose to do with their education and whether or not to expand on it, so the last chapter of this book isn't really meant to be chronologically considered. Choosing colleges, trade schools, or taking time off to work or intern is something that should be discussed well before graduation. Many of these opportunities need to be applied for and set up during or even before students' senior year. Even so, these paths all branch off into their own different directions, so let's take a deep breath and try not to worry too much about the future.

Whatever homeschooled students choose to take on next will be sought with the love and lessons that came from home. That is such a comforting fact. Home educators don't have to stop teaching. They should always be there for guidance and can even keep helping out with co-ops and other community organizations if they so desire, but they have to give their graduates the opportunity to go out and prove just how well they were taught and use that education to become the adults we've been preparing them to be.

We build our house of education, and then we hope our children will go on to create their own constructs. Graduation is an end and a beginning. So, let's get to the end of this book and hopefully prepare you and your children for new beginnings.

EARLY ADULTHOOD: GRADUATION / COLLEGE / TRADE SCHOOLS / TAKING TIME OFF / JOB PROSPECTS

S tudents form their own idea of graduation and what to do afterward based on their experiences and the influence of their parents. Homeschooled students especially (thankfully) have more options than ever. Gone are the days when being homeschooled is a questionable situation. Now that home education has expanded, and parents have more resources than ever, we are also able to give our children the best sendoff into young adulthood.

Sometimes, this includes a different timeline than the standard graduation age. Sometimes, it follows age-related tradition perfectly. The maturity of our students and their goals are what determines this. From there, graduation and what to do next continues.

Not every student wants a lavish graduation ceremony. Some look forward to a party to celebrate this great accomplishment. However parents choose to fulfill their duties as mothers, fathers, and home educators, it doesn't change the fact that the future successes of their children are contingent upon not just graduation but the opportunities sought and sized up afterward.

College degree programs, trade schools, and job offers all lead down different paths. None is better than any other, depending on circumstance. Some do cost more than others, but that never ensures success either, so it's essential for ourselves, our children, and the budgets that we take careful consideration and counsel our kids to make good, solid decisions regarding their education and how to apply it once they graduate.

Early adulthood is full of uncertainties. It can be overwhelming at times but no more than any other pivotal point in life. Homeschooled students will find their way even if they make a bad decision because they're young and have more time to change their minds and try something new if things don't work out. (I keep reminding myself of this to quell my own personal fears).

One of the main decisions home educators and students need to make—as children near young adulthood—is what timeline they are seeking. Some students benefit from accelerated learning programs that prepare them for early graduation. It's a great prospect for studious scholars. It's better for mature students that are more level-headed.

My eldest has been looking forward to this for years. She is very grounded and easily focused. Her hope is to earn her way early because she wishes to get married and have children sooner than most women do nowadays, yet she wishes to gain some real-life experience first and potentially start her own business as well. When learning about long, drawn-out college degree programs that span four to six or even eight years, her hopes of mothering a large family with a good education and well-rounded work experience seemed a bit out of reach.

Her dreams are contingent on many factors, but one, in particular, is proper timing. Parents have to use their better judgment to gauge what works for each child. Knowing my daughter and her mannerisms, I have no doubt that she can achieve most, if not all of her dreams. Because of this, she is two grades ahead and scheduled to graduate at the age of 16.

Her college fund is set to mature at this time and was designed to follow her specific timeline. This is where budgeting is incredibly helpful. My husband and I have opened college funds for each of our children through Gerber Life Insurance (131). This was the best option for our family. Instead of hosting our own savings accounts—which can easily be tapped into in case of an emergency, or when our house needs work—we found that paying into a college fund through the Gerber Life program keeps college more secure. Each college fund is paid monthly, like a bill, and has a set date for maturity, where the fixed amount allotted will be paid out.

This is not the only route. Plenty of parents open simple savings accounts, CDs, or other college funds and find them to be useful. There's always the old standby, burying a jar of money in the backyard too, but watch out for moles and rabbit holes. All joking aside, some parents don't feel the need to help their children pay for college, and that's another option as well. Plenty of college students learn fiscal responsibility by working their way through school. I was definitely on my own when it came to work and higher education, and I've done very well for myself.

I'm also a summer baby. Being so, I turned eighteen right before my senior year of high school and was older than a lot of the students graduating with me. Although I believe I would have benefitted from graduating earlier, turning nineteen the summer after I graduated didn't hinder me, and some students may actually benefit from a later graduation. Because homeschoolers can graduate students on their own timeline, young adults who struggle with lessons and the pressure of graduating can take extra time. If they feel the need to receive an extra semester or two at home, parents can give them the extended schooling they need to receive the education that best prepares them for what comes next.

It may not be ideal, and plenty of parents may balk at the idea, but everyone learns at different rates and education is not a race. Students born early in the school year may find it much more promising to slow down and take their time. Maybe they need to be closer to nineteen years old to fully comprehend their studies, or maybe a few more months will boost their confidence.

Late graduation affords home educators the opportunity to further build up college funds, or help students learn money management skills as they take their time finalizing their homeschooling career. However this is realized, all budgets can be adjusted accordingly, parents can meet their children's needs, and students can move on with the tools they need to embrace self-reliance.

Once students have made the grade and passed all of their homeschool courses, graduation options are plenty. As mentioned in the co-op chapter, parents can pay to have their students walk with their peers in a traditional ceremony celebrating their accomplishments. Some home educators host their own graduation ceremonies as well (132). This is a self-funded effort that can be as simple as a backyard get-together or as lavish as the biggest private part involving hired speakers and other special guests (133).

Students can prepare speeches. Parents can create slide shows. A lot of homeschoolers combine their graduation ceremonies with a graduation party after wards. It's a special time for parents and their children. Sticking to a budget can be especially hard during this last step because we sometimes want to splurge on extras to reward our students. In order to avoid over-spending and ending up severely in the red, I highly suggest planning for this event over the course of at least a year. Even opening a special account dedicated to graduation alone, much like a college fund, is a good idea to keep everything on track. And because I have four kids, I have to say, never underestimate the power of dollar stores and resale shops—especially when throwing a large party.

Now, some homeschooled students don't want all the fuss. They've had a small, quiet education compared to the overcrowding and extended hours that children in the public education system face. Not every student wants a ceremony or even a party for that manner. It may be hard for some home educators to grasp, and compromises may need to be made, but finding a balance and even embracing a student's wish to graduate without a giant party saves parents money and allows them to move on without tears or apprehensions.

I know I've spent a good deal of pages discussing my children, especially my eldest, but that's because teaching them specifically has given me much insight. Of course, my shy, reserved, studious oldest child doesn't want a graduation ceremony or even a party. She's already stated this time and time again. It's a topic that frequently enters her mind, and she feels very strongly about it.

As a mother, I wish to respect her desires because her education is ultimately *her* journey, but I do struggle with it at times. I want to be the proud parent clapping and cheering for her. Even so, I also know that she would appreciate a simple dinner with just her immediate family without any mention of her past, present, or future. That's just how she is. She doesn't need all the celebratory gestures.

I half-blame myself because I didn't walk when I graduated from community college, and she's always been curious about this fact. That experience also helps me to better understand her position. When I graduated with my AA, I just wanted to keep going and never look back. I finally got my butt in gear and finished college right after my second daughter was born. I was pregnant and gave birth during that last semester, but I finished. Somehow I made it.

My eldest has so many hopes and dreams, so many goals and plans that the thought of stopping to have a party seems overwhelming and counter-productive. She doesn't want it to slow her down. Graduation ceremonies and parties aren't likely to slow everyone down, but they can make the gravity of the situation weigh more heavily. Students who wish to avoid that are well within their rights. Parents who work hard to educate their children deserve their proper due. Somewhere in between, homeschooled graduates who want to avoid the big finish will hopefully find common ground with doting parents, or maybe the roles are reversed at times.

My youngest daughter is pretty young and not close enough to graduation to really worry about it yet, but she is adamant that she wants the ceremony and party with all the trimmings. She's also an extrovert. She loves meeting new people and being social, so it fits her personality.

Each kid needs to be treated differently, just as each family has to do what they feel is best. Parents who don't have the resources to pay for graduation ceremonies or parties may be satisfied with getting their children to the end of their high school education and wish to leave it at that. There are plenty of standpoints and lifestyles that different homeschooling families lead. Being self-funded puts all the pressure on homeschooling parents. Our budget fuels everything our children learn. Yes, there are plenty of deals we can take advantage of along the way, but homeschooling on a budget does present a stronger need to map out paths and follow them with stricter visions.

Most home educators help their kids figure out what they wish to do after graduation long before the big day. It seems so eminent. Students with college funds may feel obligated to further their education, but in my house, my kids know that if they chose to follow a different path that their funds will be waiting to help if-and-when they decide to start a business, buy a car, get an apartment, or maybe just learn how to make totally awesome pickles and run a booth at the farmer's market.

My mom tried to give me a good start, but things just didn't work out that way. When I graduated high school, my college fund had about $50 in it, and I needed that to pay for utilities in the apartment I shared with my sister and our roommate. I tried my hand at many jobs and learned through experience and failure. Somehow, I fell into writing and journalism, and everything worked out.

Everyone's story is different. We all find our way, and quite often, the path seems predestined. Faith and family are the guiding lights that lead us through darkness once we move out on our own. Education is a seemingly long journey, but it's one that takes us through childhood into our adult years. Just being able to teach our children, filling them with values and the passion they deserve is miraculous. The point is, if you save enough to give your kids a good homeschool education when they're young, they'll be better off with or without a college fund or a graduation party.

Students who aren't quite sure about going off to college but wish to further their education have a few options. Community college is a great stepping-stone for students who remain living at home that wish to work toward a higher-education degree. There's a multitude of programs available, but the most universally exported and widely received by four-year colleges is the Associate of the Arts. It's a general studies degree that gets the core classes out of the way so if and when students transfer onward, they can focus their time and money on courses focused on their specific field of study.

Community college is a simple option that allows students to save money while they work toward a degree program. They're also a perfect place for students to build up activities and good grades to apply for scholarships that can pay for more expensive degree programs should they choose to transfer and earn a bachelor's degree, master's, or PhD. When I went to St. Louis Community College, I had a wonderful English teacher who shared a helpful scholarship resource. It's a book called *How to Go to College Almost for Free: The Secrets of Winning Scholarship Money*, and it's still a helpful resource today—one which is ready for my children. Within the pages, this book not only details lists of college scholarships just waiting to be applied to but how to write essays that will win the money.

Community colleges offer a lot of great resources and information like this, yet, unfortunately, some of these schools have become increasingly politically biased in recent years, so parents and young adults wishing to pursue academic studies over woke ideologies, or culturally responsive, racially-charged identity requirements may find difficulty, as many community colleges now require sensitivity training as a graduation requirement, but that all depends on the state. In Eastern Missouri, St. Louis Community College (134) and St. Charles Community College (135), programs are not only still reasonable, but Missouri Senate Bill 997, implemented in 2018, requires all general education courses to be accepted across every public college in the state.

How other states compare is up to their legislation, but that's good news being that when bills like this are successful, other states are likely to follow suit. Policies of this nature encourage community college students to get their AA degree and then transfer straight to a four-year college without having to retake core classes or lose their credits. This is an added incentive, especially for homeschooled students who often utilize community college as a stepping-stone to ease themselves into a larger classroom setting.

For homeschooled students who feel prepared to go straight into a four-year college, that is another promising path. It can be a great opportunity to branch out and seek training in an important field. Making sure that students enter well sought out fields with plenty of hiring potential is key. This stretches college money further because tuition is paid back faster as students graduate, obtain the career placement they desire, and earn a fulfilling living that pays well.

Again, in recent times, colleges have taken a quite liberal bent on degree programs. They offer more classes with little to no real-world work potential than ever, and so, there are plenty of graduates left without proper prospects. Sure, art history classes helped me appreciate history better, but it served me better as an elective than it would have as a full-blown degree program because there is only so much a person can do with an art history degree. From gender studies to cultural responsibility, there is an ongoing list of seemingly useless degree programs being added to college rosters every year. Homeschoolers are well aware of this, and most of us are smart enough to steer our kids away from these expensive traps, but one of the best ways to avoid the pitfalls altogether is to seek conservative colleges.

Conservative colleges are more studies-focused. They don't pander to one-sided politics nearly as much as liberal colleges. Best of all, parents can rest easy knowing that they're supporting their children to make better choices rather than sending them off to schools that serve as socialist factories that, frankly, spend more time decrying hard work than they do instilling knowledge.

Now, this book is about budgeting, not politics, but home educators who wish to save money and help their children must be aware of certain truths. Many of us have turned to homeschooling to avoid failing school systems and damaging public school ideologies or policies while providing a balanced, loving educational environment. Once they move on to college, we cannot provide that directly, but we can indirectly set our students up for success by weeding out schools that fight against our values and ideals.

Homeschooling in itself is a more conservative concept. It sticks to a stricter budget, more individualized learning with an emphasis on personal responsibility, and traditional values that don't shy away from faith and family. This doesn't have to be held as some exclusionary red tape, however. Anyone can and should homeschool if it suits them, yet those of us who started homeschooling years ago or are beginning just now because of the widespread failures and inconsistencies that plague the public education system must acknowledge that liberal colleges have many more problems than the public schools we have escaped. Conservative colleges will have their own drawback, I'm sure, but there is a lot to consider, especially if you've built up a substantial college fund because we're footing the bill, and our dollars are truly our own real vote.

To save parents time and maybe a bit of money, I've found a couple of lists of the most conservative colleges. The first survey is specifically based on colleges that do not pander to or promote socialism (136). It's a top-fifty list that I've noted in the resources at the back of the book, and I will only detail the first five to save space and keep this chapter from lasting forever and putting everyone to sleep. (We do have children to teach, after all.) The top five from this list are Hillsdale College, Grove City College, College of the Ozarks, Liberty College, and Colorado Christian University.

The second list of conservative colleges that I found to be helpful surveyed students and ranked colleges by their student body's political affiliation (137). By this measure, the top five conservative colleges are Brigham Young University, Cedarville University, Bob Jones University, and Liberty University. There are plenty more on this list as well, so parents and students can check them out together or on their own.

For homeschooled students who don't feel that college is a right fit, trade schools are increasing in popularity. Learning a useful trade is a perfect way to gain valuable skills that can be directly applied to a well-paying position in a useful, in-demand field. Whether students are working toward becoming an electrician, carpenter, or even a beautician, trade schools get students trained and employed faster than typical college programs.

Not to sound too much like a commercial, but I have a great respect for hard-working individuals who go to a vocational school. Technical schools or vocational programs are perfect for people who like to learn fast and work with their hands. My youngest daughter loves doing hair. She wants to become a hair stylist when she grows up and dreams of going to beauty school so she can do fancy updos for weddings and other special events.

If either or both of my sons wish to go into plumbing or some other useful trade, I will wholly support that because those are the careers that pay well and are always in demand. There is so much to be said for respecting the people who keep our infrastructure running properly. Plus, it's a good living that can easily be expanded on.

Each schooling option has various completion levels. Community colleges, four-year universities, and trade schools offer certificates and degrees. These vary in price and effort required. Looking at the short and long-term benefits of each option is helpful. Some lower-cost certificates don't have as much training or growth level as degrees; some degree programs seem nearly identical to certificates yet are way more costly.

Every aspect of education comes with choices that eventually have to be made. Students facing homeschool graduation and what comes next are often unsure of what's best and so home educators have the added bonus of having a closer connection with their children because they have taken such an active role in their learning process, and that affords them a little more input. Homeschooling parents aren't just respected as mothers and fathers by their children but also as teachers and guides. That bond is priceless.

Sometimes, that bond is tested when students chose to take time off after graduation or go straight to work. Time off is a good idea for some. It gives students an adjustment period to mature and gain work experience. I took a year off before I went to college, and that wasn't enough. I ended up quitting after my first community college semester and didn't go back until years later when I finally set my mind on graduation.

I wasn't homeschooled, and I didn't have a lot of guidance, either. Again, circumstances and individual goals matter. A year off can seem like a long time to homeschooling parents who are watching their teenage son or daughter look at their future with uncertainty. Some students take that time and then get motivated. Some get comfortable in the workforce and don't ever return to the classroom.

What drives their success isn't a pile of money to pay for supplies and courses. It isn't even the tightest budget in the state. Homeschooled students find their way when they are encouraged to do what's best for them. This, of course, must be balanced.

If one of my children suddenly decides they want to be a snake charmer, I'll have some questions for sure. I'll definitely want to meet the snake. Most importantly, I won't just hand over their entire college fund just because they decided they know what they want to do. Making wise monetary decisions throughout our children's lives displays how to properly conserve and utilize money. Our children learn best through example, and though they may deviate from whatever plans we make with and/or for them, we need to keep that in mind.

That being said, plenty of successful businessmen and enterprising women have been able to build national companies from the ground up. Students who wish to go into business for themselves can research, create a plan, and go for it. Looking at some American success stories, Richard Branson didn't even finish high school (138). Debbi Fields, of Mrs. Fields Cookies, was a housewife with no business experience when she started her company (139). Frank Lloyd Wright never finished high school (140) but obtained a job working for the dean at the University of Wisconsin and was afforded to take classes there under special circumstances (141). He went on to not only work as an architect without any degrees but is still considered the greatest American architect of all time.

Time off can be just as productive as any other endeavor, so long as young adults have some direction and responsibilities. Plenty of small businesses are started and run by individuals who had an idea and nothing more. My father-in-law was one of those people. He loved motorcycles and when it was time to grow up and have a family, he decided he was going to be his own boss and build and fix up motorcycles and sell them. Midwest Cycle Salvage (142) has been a standard in Green Bay, Wisconsin for decades.

As parents, we budget and plan and hope. We do what we can to help our kids grow and learn so they're prepared to handle living on their own. Sometimes that means packing them off to college and leaving them with all the love we can give. Sometimes that means redirecting their college fund into a business venture.

Going straight to work isn't easy, but neither is sitting in boring lectures all day. I worked double shifts every weekend and spent weeknights working to support myself through my last semester of high school, and when that was finally done, I worked two and three jobs to support myself. That work gave me resilience and a stronger appreciation for free time. It also taught me how to work better and plan for bigger, more substantial goals.

Students who wish to enter the workforce right after high school can and will achieve success if they apply themselves. They can learn as they go and "climb ladders," as the saying goes. Best of all, occasionally, there are the self-motivated individuals who have a vision so clear and so passionate that they are able to start their own business with little to no experience and turn it into a massive success.

This is not solely based on chance, nor is it something home educators should bank on, but remember to step back, offer support, and contemplate what kind of investment we have already put into our child's education, as this process will help us to decide what kind of support we can offer. Whether it's just a pat on the back, being your kid's first customer, or helping to secure a food truck or a retail location, these routes are all possible with a good budget and a plan

That's all it takes. Homeschoolers can budget for anything. We can get our children through any grade. Whether we teach from kindergarten through high school graduation or just for a year or two, the time and effort we put into our children with a sound budget and serious care remains with them for the rest of their lives.

The end of each home education story has a lot to say about hard work and dedication. Though the details are different, once our children finish their studies at home, they have plenty more to learn. Some graduate early or late. Some students go straight to community colleges, significant universities, or trade schools. Others find work or even start their own businesses.

There is no end to a good education because learning is a never-ending process, but eventually, parents will no longer have to scrimp and save for supplies. In time, teaching materials are merely nostalgic symbols of the work we put in. Homeschooling may seem scary and strenuous at the start for some, or exciting and new for others, but eventually our budgets pull us through and we get our children to their next venture. It's an unparalleled experience for everyone involved.

CLOSING THOUGHTS

Homeschooling isn't easy. No educational process should be. Learning is about growth and accepting challenges—molding minds and giving students the ability to not only think for themselves but DO for themselves as well.

I love teaching. When I first started homeschooling, I was terrified. I didn't know anyone else who was educating their children at home. But I did my homework. I tested methods and did everything I could to have fun with my children as I taught them, all while our family changed and grew over time. I'm not special. Anyone can do what I've done, and I hope you do.

There's no single way to impart knowledge. Teaching isn't only successful when "experts" stand before a group of kids and lecture them. Regardless of what the Department of Education, your neighbors, or any number of skeptical family members say, parents can and do give their children the best education possible every day. More and more are doing so as these pages turn.

Whether you have older children who just aren't doing well in the system, you've got young kids who are just starting out, you're pregnant, or you're just curious about the possibilities for when you do have kids, homeschooling is a viable option with countless success stories. This book was written by someone who was raised poor—someone who was once homeless (for a brief span). I know what it means to go without, but none of that hindered my ability to learn or teach. Education doesn't have to be expensive. There are plenty of free and affordable teaching resources for parents and students who are struggling, and you don't have to be "barely scraping by" to utilize them. Even if you're a middle-class parent—or upper-class—the methods I presented can help save money when homeschooling to open up funding for other prospects.

However you use the information given, I hope it benefits you and your children. Everyone deserves the opportunity to learn and teach as they see fit. Homeschooling on a budget is just another education option. Like public school and private school, teaching at home is an opportunity that can benefit children and their families based on their individualized needs. It's as simple as that.

ACKNOWLEDGMENTS

My partner in crime has to be mentioned right away. My husband, Dash, is a man of many talents, and he truly didn't believe that teaching could be one of them. Yet, somehow, he continues to help me educate our four children through floods (which left our basement classroom looking more like a public pool than a place of learning), tornados (a tree was literally dropped onto our home and landed in just the perfect spot to mess up the exterior of the roof and nothing more), and plenty of busted sinks, leaky pipes, and fried electrical circuits.

My sister always marvels at how I can squeeze a dollar out of rocks. She has always told me how my budgeting skills are like magic, and that amazement is helpful when you're having to cut back on groceries to survive. My mom was the first person to teach me that learning never ends and that it should be fun. My in-laws, (Uncle Nate and the Gulmire crowd: especially Grandma Kate, Grandpa Dan, and Aunt Nikki) deserve some credit as well, just for having to deal with our year-round schooling schedule and our strict policies against spoiling children too much.

The lovely S.H.I.N.E. community and the wonderful Cathy Mullins also deserve endless thanks for being so welcoming and informative. I'd also like to thank Defiance Press, especially Cassandra and Maxwell, for helping me get this book out there. And then, of course, I have to acknowledge my wonderful, crazy, home-circus of children. Anna, Lexi, Wyatt, and Carlin:

you amazing little (and no longer so little) people make my world a colorful happy Summerland of love and sunshine. You teach me more than I could ever teach you, and I'm just so grateful to not only be your mother but to also be your teacher and confidant as you age through all our lessons and those taught by Daddy. A lot of mothers are sad as their children age, but I'm excited. I can't wait to see what you do and how you face the world with all your unique abilities. I'm such a lucky mama . . . and one proud educator.

SOURCE LINKS

1. Chen, Grace. "An Overview of the Funding of Public Schools." Public School Review. 31 Mar 2021. Web.
    https://www.publicschoolreview.com/blog/an-overview-of-the-funding-of-public-schools

2. Research Staff. "Public School Teacher Salaries." National Education Association Rankings and Estimated database. Jun 2021. Web.
    https://ncses.nsf.gov/indicators/states/indicator/public-school-teacher-salaries

3. Research Staff. "School Superintendent Salary in the United States." Salary.com. 26 Apr 2022. Web.
    https://www.salary.com/research/salary/benchmark/school-superintendent-salary

4. Research Staff. "U.S. School Spending Per Pupil Increased for Fifth Consecutive Year, U.S. Census Bureau Reports." United States Census Bureau. 21 May 2019. Web.
    https://www.census.gov/newsroom/press-releases/2019/school-spending.html

5. Research Staff. "Average Public School Spending / Student." Public School Review. 2022. Web.
    https://www.publicschoolreview.com/average-spending-student-stats/national-data

6. Levine, Jon. "Powerful teachers union influenced CDC on school reopenings, emails show." New York Post. 1 May 2021. Web.
    https://nypost.com/2021/05/01/teachers-union-collaborated-with-cdc-on-school-reopening-emails/

7. Lungariello, Mark. "Florida school board member under fire for field trip to known gay bar." New York Post. 28 Oct 2021. Web.
    https://nypost.com/2021/10/28/florida-school-board-member-under-fire-for-bar-field-trip/

8. Colton, Emma. "California teacher boasts not having American flag, tells students to pledge allegiance to gay pride flag." Fox News. 28 Aug 2021. Web.
    https://www.foxnews.com/us/california-teacher-pledge-of-allegiance-pride-flag

9. Keene, Houston. "Schools across America implement BLM Week of Action that calls for 'disruption of Western nuclear family.'" Fox News. 2 Feb 2022. Web.
    https://www.foxnews.com/politics/schools-across-america-blm-week-action-nuclear-family

10. Gabe. "This Football Team Banned From Flying Blue Line Flag Despite Who They Were Honoring . . ." Click It Conservative News. 2020. Web.
    https://clickitconservativenews.com/this-football-team-banned-from-flying-blue-line-flag-despite-who-they-were-honoring/

11. Zwicker, Heather. "FCPS reinstates pornographic books to school libraries." Fairfax County Times. 3 Dec 2021. Web.

https://www.fairfaxtimes.com/articles/fcps-reinstates-pornographic-books-to-school-libraries/article_cf63abf2-53ab-11ec-affa-cbfc8074da6a.html

12. Baumgartner, Jessica Marie. "Hollywood, The Media, And Public Education Have Been Grooming Us For Years." Evie Magazine. 21 Jan 2022. Web. https://www.eviemagazine.com/post/hollywood-the-media-and-public-education-has-been-grooming-us-for-years

13. Associated Press. "NorCal mother alleges teachers manipulated child to change gender identity." KTLA News. 21 Jan 2021. Web. https://ktla.com/news/california/norcal-mother-alleges-teachers-manipulated-child-to-change-gender-identity/

14. Associated Press. "Parents sue Wisconsin school district over gender transition policy." 17 Nov 2021. Web. https://www.nbcnews.com/news/us-news/parents-sue-wisconsin-school-district-gender-transition-policy-rcna5965

15. Poff, Jeremiah. "Florida parents sue school district over daughter's secret gender transition." Washington Examiner. 26 Jan 2022. Web. https://www.washingtonexaminer.com/restoring-america/community-family/florida-parents-sue-school-district-over-daughters-secret-gender-transition

16. Stabile, Angelica. "Oregon lowering education standards for minority students enabling 'school to prison pipeline': Maj Toure." Fox News. 10 Aug 2021. Web. https://www.foxnews.com/media/oregon-lowering-education-standards-minority-students

17. Backes, Ben, Goldhaber, Dan & Xu, Zeyu. "Transition Intervention in High School and Pathway Through College." National Center for Analysis of Longitudinal Data in Education Research. Aug 2021. Web. https://caldercenter.org/sites/default/files/CALDER%20WP%20255-0821.pdf

18. Poff, Jeremiah. "77% of students at Baltimore high school reading at elementary levels, teacher says." Washington Examiner. 1 Feb 2022. Web. https://www.washingtonexaminer.com/policy/77-of-students-at-baltimore-high-school-reading-at-elementary-levels-teacher-says

19. Writing Staff. "Why Are Gifted Programs Needed?" National Association for Gifted Children. 2022. Web. https://www.nagc.org/resources-publications/gifted-education-practices/why-are-gifted-programs-needed

20. Baumgartner, Jessica Marie. "Americans Are Sacrificing Kids To Protect Adults, And It Has To Stop." Evie Magazine. 17 Jan 2022. Web. https://www.eviemagazine.com/post/americans-are-sacrificing-kids-to-protect-adults-and-it-has-to-stop

21. Tobey, John S. "Inflation And Interest Rates Rise - Fed Loses Control." Forbes. 15 Jan 2022. Web. https://www.forbes.com/sites/johntobey/2022/01/15/inflation-and-interest-rates-risefed-loses-control/?sh=2a20d0ae1763

22. Writing Staff. "Cost of Homeschooling VS Public School." Homeschool-curriculum. org. 2022. Web.
https://homeschool-curriculum.org/cost-of-homeschooling/

23. Research Staff. "Homeschool Laws by State." Home School Legal Defense Association. 2022. Web.
https://hslda.org/legal/

24. Writing Staff. "Homeschoolers in the 2019 Scripps National Spelling Bee." Homeschooling Teen. 2019. Web.
http://homeschoolingteen.com/article/homeschoolers-in-the-2019-scripps-national-spelling-bee/

25. Nielson, Euell A. "ZAILA AVANT-GARDE (2007–)." Black Past. 10 Jul, 2021. Web.
https://www.blackpast.org/african-american-history/zaila-avant-garde-2007/

26. Toledo, Bella. "15 Successful People You Didn't Know Were Homeschooled." Colour My Learning. 15 Jul 2020. Web.
https://www.colourmylearning.com/2020/07/15-successful-people-you-didnt-know-were-homeschooled/

27. TED Staff. "30 Successful People Who Were Homeschooled." Top Education Degrees. 2022. Web.
https://www.topeducationdegrees.org/successful-people-who-were-homeschooled/

28. Burnett, Christie. "Reading Without Words: The Why and How of Wordless Books." Scholastic Parents. 16 Apr 2018. Web.
https://www.scholastic.com/parents/books-and-reading/raise-a-reader-blog/reading-without-words-why-and-how-wordless-books.html

29. MacPherson, Karen. "Terrific children's books without words." The Washington Post. 26 Jun 2018. Web.
https://www.washingtonpost.com/entertainment/books/terrific-childrens-books-without-words/2018/06/22/8c139c22-6f4d-11e8-afd5-778aca903bbe_story.html

30. Writing Staff. "20 PICTURE BOOKS WITHOUT WORDS WE LOVE." Mother Magazine. 2022. Web.
https://www.mothermag.com/picture-books-without-words/

31. Brumback, Elijah. "These 10 Books Without Words Turn You Into The Master Storyteller At Bedtime." Fatherly. 15 Jul 2016. Web.
https://www.fatherly.com/play/wordless-books/

32. Writing Staff. "What is the purpose of a public library?" Public Libraries. 2022. Web.
https://publiclibraries.com/

33. Research Staff. "Homepage." U.S. Department of Education. 2022. Web.
https://www.ed.gov/

34. Parton, Dolly. "Homepage." Dolly Parton's Imagination Library. 2022. Web.
https://imaginationlibrary.com/

35. Encyclopedia Britannica Editors. "Public Broadcasting Service." Britannica. 2022. Web.
https://www.britannica.com/topic/Public-Broadcasting-Service

36. Ducharme, Jamie. "The WAHO Estimated COVID-19 Mortality at 3.4%. That Doesn't Tell the Whole Story." Time Magazine. 9 Mar 2020. Web. https://time.com/5798168/coronavirus-mortality-rate/

37. Research Staff. "Science Brief: SARS-CoV-2 and Surface (Fomite) Transmission for Indoor Community Environments." Center for Disease Control and Prevention. 5 Apr 2021. Web. https://www.cdc.gov/coronavirus/2019-ncov/more/ science-and-research/surface-transmission.html

38. Jennifer K. Bender1Comments to Author , Michael Brandl1, Michael Höhle, Udo Buchholz, and Nadine Zeitlmann. "Analysis of Asymptomatic and Presymptomatic Transmission in SARS-CoV-2 Outbreak, Germany, 2020." Center for Disease Control and Prevention. 4 Apr 2021. Web. https://wwwnc.cdc.gov/eid/article/27/4/20-4576_article

39. Goldbaum, Ellen. "UB study to investigate why COVID-19 kills some adults but barely affects children." University of Buffalo. 6 Apr 2020. Web. https://www.buffalo.edu/ubnow/stories/2020/04/hicar-covid-kids.html

40. Miltimore, Jon. "CDC: Schools With Mask Mandates Didn't See Statistically Significant Different Rates of COVID Transmission From Schools With Optional Policies." Foundation for Economic Education. 25 Aug 2021. Web. https://fee.org/articles/cdc-schools-with-mask-mandates- didn-t-see-statistically-significant-different-rates-of-covid- transmission-from-schools-with-optional-policies/

41. Li, David K. "Youth suicide attempts soared during pandemic, CDC report says." NBC News. 11 Jun 2021. Web. https://www.nbcnews.com/news/us-news/youth-suicide-attempts- soared-during-pandemic-cdc-report-says-n1270463

42. Staff. "Lone Elk Park." Saint Louis County Parks & Recreation. 2022. Web. https://stlouiscountymo.gov/st-louis-county- departments/parks/places/lone-elk-park/#FA

43. Staff. "Rockwoods Reservation." Missouri Department of Conservation. Apr 2020. Web. https://mdc.mo.gov/sites/default/files/mo_nature/ downloads/conservation-areas/5405.pdf

44. Staff. "Cahokia Mounds." Cahokia Mounds Museum Society. 2022. Web. https://cahokiamounds.org/

45. Staff. "Fort Zumwalt Park." O'Fallon, Missouri Parks & Rec. 2022. Web. https://www.ofallon.mo.us/fort-zumwalt-park

46. Staff. "Fees And Hours, Daniel Boone Home." St. Charles County. 2022. Web. https://www.sccmo.org/1775/Fees-and-Hours

47. Staff. "Homepage." Abraham Lincoln Presidential Library and Museum. 2022. Web. https://presidentlincoln.illinois.gov/

48. Writing Staff. "Free to See: 20 U.S. Museums." National Geographic Magazine. 24 Aug 2011. Web. https://www.nationalgeographic.com/travel/article/museums-us

49. Staff. "Visit a Museum through Museums for All." Museums for All. 2022. Web.
    https://museums4all.org/

50. Staff. "Homepage." Saint Louis Art Museum. 2022. Web.
    https://www.slam.org/

51. Staff. "Homepage." The Magic House. 2022. Web.
    https://www.magichouse.org/

52. Staff. "Homepage." The Children's Museum of Green Bay. 2022. Web.
    https://gbchildrensmuseum.org/

53. Staff. "Homepage." Family Museum. 2022. Web.
    https://familymuseum.org/about

54. Staff. "Homepage." Saint Louis Zoo. 2022. Web.
    https://www.stlzoo.org

55. Staff. "Why the Wild Needs Wolves." Endangered Wolf Center. 2022. Web.
    https://www.endangeredwolfcenter.org/

56. Staff. "Explore World Bird Sanctuary." World Bird Sanctuary. 2022. Web.
    https://www.worldbirdsanctuary.org/

57. Staff. "Welcome To The Y." YMCA. 2022. Web.
    https://www.ymca.org/

58. Staff. "Find a Club near you." Boys & Girls Clubs of America. 2022. Web.
    https://www.bgca.org/get-involved/find-a-club

59. Loannidis, John P.A. "The infection fatality rate of COVID-19 inferred from
    seroprevalence data." BML Yale. 2022. Web.
    https://www.medrxiv.org/content/10.1101/2020.05.13.20101253v1

60. Staff. "SHARE St. Louis Homeschooling, Activities, Resources, & Encouragement."
    Homeschool-life. 2022. Web.
    https://www.homeschool-life.com/mo/share/

61. Baumgartner, Jessica Marie. "St. Louis Homeschool Pioneer Details Her Journey
    Through Teaching." The Epoch Times. 17 Aug 2021. Web.
    https://www.theepochtimes.com/st-louis-homeschool-pioneer-
    details-her-journey-through-teaching_3952584.html

62. Staff. "SHINE St. Charles." Homeschool-life. 2022. Web.
    https://www.homeschool-life.com/2522/

63. Staff. "Why Choose Homeschool-Life.com?" Homeschool-Life. 2022. Web.
    https://www.homeschool-life.com/

64. Staff. "History of the Missouri State Penitentiary." Missouri State Penitentiary. 2022.
    Web.
    https://www.missouripentours.com/history/

65. Staff. "Homepage." Foundry Art Center. 2022. Web.
    http://foundryartcentre.org/

66. Staff. "Homepage." Great Homeschool Conventions." 2022. Web.
    https://greathomeschoolconventions.com/

67. Staff. "Culture Is Coming." Brave Books. 2022. Web.
https://bravebooks.us/

68. Staff. "Homepage." Chicken Scratch Books. 2022. Web.
https://chickenscratchbooks.com/

69. Staff. "Homepage." Christian Focus Publications. 2022. Web.
https://www.christianfocus.com/

70. Staff. "Homepage." YWAM Publishing. 2022. Web.
https://www.ywampublishing.com/

71. Staff. "Homepage." Discovery toys. 2022. Web.
https://www.discoverytoys.net/

72. Staff. "Homepage." Knowledge Crate. 2022. Web.
https://www.knowledgecrates.com/

73. Staff. "Homepage." Melissa & Doug. 2022. Web.
https://www.melissaanddoug.com/

74. Staff. "Free Literature Units for Homeschooling." New Classics Study Guides. 2022. Web.
https://www.newclassicsstudyguides.com/

75. Maunz, Mary Ellen. "Montessori for Homeschooling. Age of Montessori. 2022. Web.
https://ageofmontessori.org/homeschooling

76. Staff. "Homepage." American School. 2022. Web.
https://www.americanschoolofcorr.com/

77. Staff. "You're Their First Teacher. Be Their Best Teacher." Classical Conversations. 2022. Web.
https://classicalconversations.com/

78. Staff. "What is Classical Education?" Memoria Press. 2022. Web.
https://www.memoriapress.com/

79. Staff. "Homepage." The Etiquette Factory. 2022. Web.
https://www.theetiquettefactory.com/

80. Staff. " Homepage." Growing Healthy Homes. 2022. Web.
https://growinghealthyhomes.com/

81. Staff. "Homepage." Sarah's Spanish School. 2022. Web.
https://www.sarahsspanishschool.com/

82. Staff. "Homepage." First Frets. 2022. Web.
https://firstfrets.com/

83. Staff. "Get Out and Play." United States Tennis Association. 2022. Web.
https://www.usta.com/en/home.html

84. Staff. "Homepage." St. Louis Patriots Homeschool Boys Basketball. 2022. Web.
https://stlpatriots.org/

85. Staff. "Welcome to the Panther Family." St. Louis Panthers Volleyball. 2022. Web.
https://stlpanthersvolleyball.com/

86. Staff. "Homepage." Stoa Christian Homeschool Speech and Debate. 2022. Web.
https://stoausa.org/

87. Staff. "Experienced. Nonpartisan. Defending Your Rights." Foundation For Individual Rights In Education. 2022. Web.
https://www.thefire.org/

88. Staff. "Homepage." Special Needs Tutors. 2022. Web.
https://specialneedstutors.com/

89. Baumgartner, Jessica Marie. "Yale Defends Students Who Tried To Fight A Conservative For Debating." Go 2 Tutors. Mar 2022. Web.
https://go2tutors.com/yale-law-school-threats/

90. Wood, Peter W. "Harvard cancels a black academic who debunked woke orthodoxy." New York Post. 25 Mar 2022. Web.
https://nypost.com/2022/03/25/harvard-cancels-a-black-academic-who-debunked-woke-orthodoxy/

91. Staff. "Homepage." Simpson University. 2022. Web.
https://www.simpsonu.edu/#gsc.tab=0

92. Staff. "Welcome to Harding." Harding University. 2022. Web.
https://www.harding.edu/

93. Staff. "Do College Differently." Momentous College. 2022. Web.
https://www.momentous.world/

94. Staff. "Homepage." Cub Creek Science Camp. 2022. Web.
https://cubcreeksciencecamp.com/

95. Staff. "Explore World Bird Sanctuary." World Bird Sanctuary. 2022. Web.
https://www.worldbirdsanctuary.org/

96. Staff. "Homepage." Trail Life. 2022. Web.
https://www.traillifeusa.com/

97. Swain, Carol M. "Award Winning Author." Carol M. Swain. 2022. Web.
https://carolmswain.com/books/

98. Carlson, Tucker. "The sworn enemy of censorship." Tucker Carlson. 2022. Web.
https://tuckercarlson.com/

99. Staff. "CEO Salary Email." Unicef USA. 2022. Web.
https://www.unicefusa.org/about/faq/ceo-salary-email

100. Writing Staff. "Humane Society CEO Makes $400,000, While Animals Get Screwed." Humane Watch. 20 Sept 2020. Web.
https://humanewatch.org/humane-society-ceo-makes-400000-while-animals-get-screwed/

101. Staff. "Adoption Fees." Humane Society of Missouri. 2022. Web.
https://www.hsmo.org/adoptionfees/

102. Staff. "Homepage." Open Door Animal Sanctuary. 2022. Web.
https://odas.org/

103. Staff. "About Us." Black Cat Rescue. 2022. Web.
http://blackcatrescue.com/about-us/

104. Staff. "Homepage." Stray Rescue of Saint Louis. 2022. Web.
https://www.strayrescue.org/

105. Kish, Matthew. "Goodwill CEO's salary rises again." Portland Business Journal. 15 Nov 2013. Web.
https://www.bizjournals.com/portland/print-edition/2013/11/15/goodwill-ceos-salary-rises-again.html

106. Staff. "The Society of St. Vincent de Paul." St. Vincent de Paul. 2022. Web.
https://ssvpusa.org/

107. Staff. "Executive Director/CEO." Center for Nonprofit Excellence. 2022. Web.
https://engage.cnpe.org/jobs/record/5000y00001rpTbVAAU

108. Staff. "Every Child Deserves to Be Safe and Happy." Saint Louis Crisis Nursery. 2022. Web.
https://www.crisisnurserykids.org/

109. Staff. "Homepage." Birthright. 2022. Web.
https://birthright.org/

110. Baumgartner, Jessica Marie. "Many Public Schools Dropping To 4 Days A Week In 2022-2023." Go 2 Tutors. Mar 2022. Web.
https://go2tutors.com/public-school-4-day-week/

111. Hogan, Larry. "Governor Hogan Announces Elimination of Four-Year Degree Requirement For Thousands of State Jobs." Office of the Governor. 2022. Web.
https://governor.maryland.gov/2022/03/15/governor-hogan-announces-elimination-of-four-year-degree-requirement-for-thousands-of-state-jobs/

112. Legislative Council Staff. "Fiscal Note." State of Colorado. 2022. Web.
https://leg.colorado.gov/sites/default/files/documents/2022A/bills/fn/2022a_sb140_00.pdf

113. Staff. "Work Certificates and Work Permits." Missouri Department of Labor & Industrial Relations. 2022. Web.
https://labor.mo.gov/DLS/YouthEmployment/work_cert_permit#workpermit

114. Staff. "Youth Employment for Employers." Missouri Department of Labor & Industrial Relations. 2022. Web.
https://labor.mo.gov/DLS/YouthEmployment/for_employers

115. Gonzales, Rick. "Full List Of Colleges No Longer Requiring SAT Or ACT Scores." Go 2 Tutors. Jan 2022. Web.
https://go2tutors.com/colleges-no-sat-or-act-scores/

116. Writing Staff. "50 Successful People Who Have a GED." Gedno. 6 Feb 2022. Web.
https://gedeno.com/50-successful-people-ged/

117. Writing Staff. "SAT vs ACT: Which Test is Right for You?" The Princeton Review. 2022. Web.
https://www.princetonreview.com/college/sat-act

118. Nietzel, Michael T. "California State University Ends Use Of SAT, ACT For Undergraduate Admissions." Forbes. 24 Mar 2022. Web.
https://www.forbes.com/sites/michaeltnietzel/2022/03/24/california-state-university-ends-use-of-sat-act-for-undergraduate-admissions/

119. Silva, Daniella. "After MIT reinstates SAT and ACT mandate, will other colleges follow?" NBC News. 30 Mar 2022. Web. https://www.msn.com/en-us/news/us/after-mit-reinstates-sat-and-act-mandate-will-other-colleges-follow/ar-AAVFokw

120. Staff. "Downloadable Full-Length Practice Tests." SAT Suite of Assessment. 2022. Web. https://satsuite.collegeboard.org/sat/practice-preparation/practice-tests

121. Staff. "ACT Official Subject Guides—2nd Edition." ACT. 2022. Web. https://www.act.org/content/act/en/products-and-services/the-act/test-preparation/act-subject-guides.html

122. Staff. "Test Fees." SAR Suite of Assessments. 2022. Web. https://satsuite.collegeboard.org/sat/registration/fees-refunds/test-fees

123. Staff. "Current ACT Fees and Services." ACT. 2022. Web. https://www.act.org/content/act/en/products-and-services/the-act/registration/fees.html

124. Staff. "Myths About Homeschool Diplomas." Let's Homeschool High School. 2022. Web. https://letshomeschoolhighschool.com/homeschool-high-school-diploma-online/

125. Staff. "Free Online High School for Specific Students" Lets Homeschool High School. 2022. Web. https://letshomeschoolhighschool.com/2013/02/24/free-online-high-school-state/

126. Staff. "Personalized High School Diploma for Homeschools." Homeschool Diploma. 2022. Web. https://www.homeschooldiploma.com/personalized-high-school-diploma-for-homeschools.html

127. Staff. "Price & State Rules." GED Testing Service. 2022. Web. https://ged.com/about_test/price_and_state_rules/

128. Staff. "Missouri HiSET® Exam Requirements." HiSET. 2022. Web. https://hiset.ets.org/requirements/state/mo/?WT.ac=hiset_34809_requirements_mo_160915

129. Staff. "High School Equivalency. "Missouri Department of Elementary & Secondary Education. 2022. Web. https://dese.mo.gov/college-career-readiness/high-school-equivalency

130. Staff. "New Online Proctored GED® Test Webinar for Educators." GED Testing Service. 2022. Web. https://ged.com/insession/new-op-ged-test-webinar_aug2020/

131. Staff. "Saving for College." Gerber Life Insurance. 2022. Web. https://www.gerberlife.com/saving-for-college

132. Sonlight. "Homeschool Graduation: How to Make it Special for Your Student." Homeschool Giveaways & Freebies. 3 Feb 2022. Web. https://homeschoolgiveaways.com/2022/02/homeschool-graduation/

133. Writing Staff. "Guide to Homeschool Graduation." Homechool.com. 2022. Web. https://www.homeschool.com/articles/guide-to-homeschool-graduation/

134. Staff. "General Education Course Requirements." St. Louis Community College Catalog. 2022. Web.
https://catalog.stlcc.edu/general-education/

135. Staff. "General Education Requirements." St. Charles Community College. 2022. Web.
https://www.stchas.edu/academics/college-catalog/gen-ed-requirements

136. Writing Staff. "Top 50 Conservative Colleges." Stopping Socialism. 23 Nov 2020. Web.
https://stoppingsocialism.com/2020/11/top-50-conservative-colleges/

137. Writing Staff. "2022 Most Conservative Colleges in America." Niche Best Colleges. 2022. Web.
https://www.niche.com/colleges/search/most-conservative-colleges/

138. Connley, Courtney. "Richard Branson says the key to success isn't a university degree." 29 Nov 2017. Web.
https://www.cnbc.com/2017/11/29/richard-branson-says-the-key-to-success-isnt-a-university-degree.html

139. Former Contributor. "How To Build A Multimillion-Dollar Company: The Story Of Mrs. Fields Cookies." Forbes. 20 Nov 2012. Web.
https://www.forbes.com/sites/learnvest/2012/11/20/how-to-build-a-multimillion-dollar-company-the-story-of-mrs-fields-cookies/?sh=19c25b4d467e

140. Writing Staff. "Frank Lloyd Wright." The Art Story. 2022. Web.
https://www.theartstory.org/artist/wright-frank-lloyd/life-and-legacy/

141. Writing Staff. "The Life of Frank Lloyd Wright." Frank Lloyd Wright Foundation. 2022. Web.
https://franklloydwright.org/frank-lloyd-wright/

142. Staff. "About Us." Midwest Cycle Salvage. 2022. Web.
https://www.ebay.com/str/midwestcyclesalvage?mkevt=1&mkcid=1&mkrid=711-53200-19255-0&campid=5336728181&customid=&toolid=10001

BIBLIOGRAPHY

Adamson, Joy. "Born Free." Pantheon Anniversary Edition. 16 Mar 2000. Print.

Beah, Ishmael. "A Long Way Gone: Memoirs of a Boy Soldier. Sarah Crichton Books. 5 Aug 2008. Print.

Berenstain, Jan & Mike. "The Berenstain Bears 12-Book Phonics Fun!" Harper Collins Box Edition. 25 Jun 2013. Print.

Bronte, Charlotte. "Jane Eyre." Wordsworth Editions Ltd. 31 Aug 1997. Print.

Burn, Doris. "Andre Henry's Meadow." Philomel Books. 5 July 2012. Print.

Burnett, Frances Hodgson. "The Secret Garden." Classics Made easy. 17 Aug 2020. Print.

Carle, Eric. "The Very Hungry Caterpillar." World of Eric Carle. 23 Mar 1994. Print.

Cronk, Harold. "The Beard Ballad." Perfect Image. 2018. Print.

Dahl, Roald. "Matilda." Puffin Books. 1 Sept 2016. Print.

Dr. Seuss. "Hop On Pop." Random House Books for Young Readers. 12 Feb 1963. Print.

Eastman, P.D. "Go Dog Go." Random House Books for Young Readers. 12 Mar 1961. Print.

Frank, Anne. "The Diary of a Young Girl." Bantam. 3 Feb 1997. Print.

Freeman, Don. "Corduroy." Viking Publishing. 1 Jan 2011. Print.

Hodegtwins. "More Than Spots & Stripes." BRAVE Books. 15 Nov 2021. Print.

Johnson, Abby. "Unplanned." Salt River. 11 Jan 2011. Print.

Kaplan, Ben. "How to Go to College Almost For Free: The Secrets of Winning Scholarship Money." Collins Reference. 18 Sept 2001. Print.

Kessler, Collen EdM. "Raising Resilient Sons." Ulysses Press. 2020. Print.

Montgomery, L.M. "Anne of Green Gables." Starfire Reprint Edition. 6 Oct 1998. Print.

Moore, Alan. "Watchmen." DC Comics. 11 Nov 2008. Print.

Mull, Brandon. "Fablehaven Series." Aladdin Boxed Set. 4 Oct 2011. Print.

North, Sterling. "Little Rascal." Scholastic. 5 Aug 1965. Print.

O'hara, Mo. "My Big Fat Zombie Goldfish." Square Fish. 11 Mar 2014. Print.

Pilkey, Dav. "Dog Man: A Graphic Novel." Graphix. 3 Aug 2021. Print.

Proimos, James III Jr. "Apocalypse Bow Wow." Bloomsbury USA Childrens. 1 Nov 2016. Print.

Rowling. J.K. "Harry Potter Series." Arthur A. Levine Books. 1 Jul 2009. Print.

Steinbeck, John. "The Grapes of Wrath." Penguin Books. 8 Jan 2002. Print.

Sterling, Dorothy. "Freedom Train: The Story of Harriet Tubman." Scholastic. 1 May 1987. Print.

Sutherland, Tui T. "Wings of Fire." Scholastic Paperbacks. 8 Sept 2015. Print.

Washington, George. "Rules of Civility & Decent Behavior In Company And Conversation." Applewood Books. 1 Aug 1989. Print.

Wilder, Laura Ingalls. "Little House Box Set." Harper Collins. 25 Oct 2016. Print.

Made in the USA
Middletown, DE
12 August 2022

70407503R10096